WHAT'S COOKING
Italian

Penny Stephens

THUNDER BAY
P · R · E · S · S

First published in the United States in 1998 by
Thunder Bay Press
An imprint of the Advantage Publishers Group
5880 Oberlin Drive, San Diego, CA 92121-4794
www.advantagebooksonline.com

Library of Congress Cataloging in Publication Data .

Stephens, Penny.
    What's cooking Italian / Penny Stephens.
        p.   cm.
    Includes Index.
    ISBN 1-57145-150-1
    1. Cookery, Italian.   I. Title
TX723. S797   1998
641.5945--dc21   98-18399
                                                        CIP

Printed in China
5 6 01 02 03

Produced by Haldane Mason, London

Acknowledgments
Art Director: Ron Samuels
Editorial Director: Sydney Francis
Editorial Consultant: Christopher Fagg
Managing Editor: Jo-Anne Cox
Editor: Lydia Darbyshire
Design: Digital Artworks Partnership Ltd
Photography: Iain Bagwell
Home Economist: Penny Stephens

Note
Unless otherwise stated, milk is assumed to be full fat, eggs are medium,
and pepper is freshly ground black pepper.

Contents

Introduction

There are two main culinary zones in Italy: the wine and olive zone, which lies around Umbria, Liguria, and the South; and the cattle country, where the olive tree will not flourish—Emilia-Romagna, Lombardy, and Veneto—but where milk and butter are widely produced. Tuscany, however, is the exception—it uses both butter and oil in its cooking because both cattle and olive trees thrive in the area.

ITALIAN FOOD REGION BY REGION

Piedmont

The food here is substantial, peasant-type fare, although the expensive fragrant white truffle is found in this region. Truffles can be finely flaked or grated and added to many of the more sophisticated dishes. There is an abundance of exotic mushrooms throughout the region. Garlic features strongly in the recipes, and polenta, gnocchi, and rice are eaten in larger quantities than pasta, the former being offered as a first course when soup is not served. A large variety of game is also widely available.

Lombardy

Milan is home to the wonderful risotto named after the city and also the Milanese soufflé flavored strongly with lemon. Veal dishes, including *vitello tonnato* and *osso buco*, are specialties of the region, and other excellent meat dishes, particularly pot roasts, feature widely. The lakes of the area produce a wealth of fresh fish. Rice and polenta are again popular, but pasta also appears in many guises. The famous sweet yeast cake *panettone* is a product of this region.

Trentino-Alto Adige

The foods are robust and basic here, where fish are plentiful. In the Trentino area particularly, pasta and simple meat dishes are popular, while in the Adige, soups and pot roasts are favored, often with added dumplings and spiced sausages.

Veneto

Polenta is served with almost everything here. The land is intensively farmed, providing mostly cereals and wine. Pasta is less in evidence, with gnocchi and rice more favored. Fish, particularly shellfish, is in abundance and especially good seafood salads are widely available. There are also excellent robust soups and risottos flavored with the seafood and sausages of the area.

Liguria

All along the Italian Riviera can be found excellent trattorias which produce amazing fish dishes flavored with the local olive oil. Pesto sauce flavored with basil, cheese, and pine nuts comes from this area, along with other excellent sauces. Fresh herbs abound, widely used in many dishes, including the famous pizzas.

Emilia-Romagna

Tortellini and lasagne feature widely here, along with many other pasta dishes, as do *saltimbocca* and other veal dishes. Parma is famous for its ham, *prosciutto di Parma*, thought to be the best in the world. Balsamic vinegar is also produced here, from wine that is distilled until it is dark brown and extremely strongly flavored.

Tuscany

Tuscany has everything: an excellent coastal area providing splendid fish, hills covered in vineyards, and fertile plains where every conceivable vegetable and fruit grows. There is plenty of game in the region, providing many interesting recipes; tripe cooked in a thick tomato sauce is popular along with many liver recipes; beans in many guises appear frequently, as well as pot roasts, steaks, and full-bodied soups, all of which are well-flavored. Florence has a wide variety of specialties, while Siena boasts the famous candied fruit cake called *Panforte di Siena*.

Umbria/Marches

Inland Umbria is famous for its pork, and the character of the cuisine is marked by the use of the local fresh ingredients, including lamb, game, and fish from the lakes. Spit-roasting and broiling is popular, and the excellent local olive oil is used both in cooking and to pour over dishes before serving. Black truffles, olives, fruit, and herbs are plentiful and feature in many recipes. First-class sausages and cured pork come from the Marches, particularly on the Umbrian border, and pasta features all over the region.

Lazio

Here, there are many pasta dishes with delicious sauces, gnocchi in various forms, and plenty of dishes featuring lamb and veal (*saltimbocca* being just one), and a variety of meats, all with plenty of herbs and seasonings giving really robust flavors and delicious sauces. Vegetables feature along with fantastic fruits; and beans appear both in soups and many other dishes.

Abruzzi and Molise

The cuisine here is deeply traditional, with local hams and cheeses from the mountain areas, interesting sausages with plenty of garlic and other seasonings, cured meats, and wonderful fish and seafood. Lamb features widely: tender, juicy, and well-flavored with herbs.

Campania

Naples is the home of pasta dishes, served with a splendid tomato sauce (with many variations). Pizza is said to have been created in Naples. Fish abounds, with *fritto misto* and *fritto pesce* being great favorites. Fish stews are robust and varied, and shellfish in particular is often served with pasta. Cutlets and steaks are excellent, served with strong sauces flavored with garlic, tomatoes, and herbs: pizzaiola steak is one of the favorites. Mozzarella cheese is produced locally and used to create the crispy Mozzarella in Carozza, again served with a garlicky tomato sauce. Sweet dishes are popular too, often with flaky pastry and ricotta cheese, and the seasonal fruit salads are laced with wine or liqueur.

Puglia (Apulia)

The ground in this region is stony, but it produces good fruit, olive groves, vegetables, and herbs, and, of course, there is a large amount of seafood from the sea. Many of the excellent pasta dishes are exclusive to the region both in shape and ingredients. Mushrooms abound and are always added to the local pizzas. Oysters and mussels are plentiful, and so is octopus. Brindisi is famous for its shellfish—both the seafood salads and risottos are truly memorable. But it is not all fish or pasta: lamb is roasted and stewed to perfection and so is veal, always with plenty of herbs.

Basilicata

Here potent wines are produced to accompany a robust cuisine largely based on pasta, lamb, pork, game, and abundant dairy products. The salami and cured meats are excellent, as are the mountain hams. Lamb is flavored with the herbs and grasses on which it feeds. Wonderful thick soups—true minestrone—are produced in the mountains, and eels and fish are plentiful in the lakes. Chilies are grown in this region and appear in many of the recipes. The cheeses are excellent, good fruit is grown, and interesting local bread is baked in huge loaves.

Calabria

This is the toe of Italy, where orange and lemon groves flourish, along with olive trees and a profusion of vegetables, especially eggplants, which are cooked in a variety of ways. Chicken, rabbit, and guinea fowl are often on the menu. Pizzas feature largely, often with a fish topping. Mushrooms grow well in the Calabrian climate and feature in many dishes from sauces and stews to salads. Pasta comes with a great variety of sauces, including baby artichokes, eggs, meat, cheese, mixed vegetables, the large sweet bell peppers of the region, and, of course, garlic. The fish is excellent, too, and fresh tuna and swordfish are available, along with many other varieties. Many desserts and cakes are flavored with aniseed, honey, and almonds and feature the plentiful figs of the region.

Sicily

This is the largest island in the Mediterranean and the cuisine is based mainly on fish and vegetables. Fish soups, stews, and salads appear in unlimited forms, including tuna, swordfish, mussels, and many more; citrus fruits are widely grown, along with almonds and pistachios, and the local wines, including the dark, sweet, dessert wine Marsala, are excellent. Meat is often given a long, slow cooking, or else is ground and shaped before cooking. Game is plentiful and is often cooked in sweet-sour sauces containing the local black olives. Pasta abounds again with more unusual sauces as well as the old favorites. All Sicilians have a love of desserts, cakes, and especially ice cream. *Cassata* and other ice creams from Sicily are famous all over the world.

Sardinia

The national dish of Sardinia is suckling pig or newborn lamb cooked on an open fire or spit, and rabbit, game, and a variety of meat dishes are also very popular. There is fresh fruit of almost every kind in abundance. Fish is also top quality, with excellent sea bass, lobsters, tuna, mullet, eels, and mussels in good supply. Myrtle (*mirto*), a local herb, is added to everything from chicken dishes to the local liqueur; and along with the cakes and breads of Sardinia, myrtle will long remain a fond memory of the island when you have returned home.

Snacks & Starters

Soups are an important part of Italian cuisine. They vary in consistency from light and delicate starters to hearty main meal soups. Although some may be puréed, the ingredients never lose their delicious flavor.

Antipasto means "before the main course" and what is served may be simple and inexpensive or highly elaborate. It usually comes in three categories: meat, fish, and vegetables. There are many varieties of cold meats, including ham, invariably sliced paper thin. All varieties of fish are enjoyed by the Italians—fresh sardines are particularly popular. Cook vegetables only until "al dente" and still slightly crisp so that they retain more nutrients and the colors remain bright.

Use plenty of color—bell peppers, snow peas, and baby corncobs are all readily available. Use Italian staples, such as extra-virgin olive oil and balsamic vinegar, for a salad dressing, and sprinkle on Italian cheeses, such as Parmesan and pecorino.

This chapter also contains a range of delicious side dishes that will complement your main meal. Whatever you are looking for to tempt those taste buds, you are sure to find it among these delicious dishes.

Tuscan Bean Soup

A thick and creamy soup that is based on a traditional Tuscan recipe.
It is delicious served with fresh, warm bread and butter.

Serves 4

INGREDIENTS

1¹/₄ cups dried lima beans soaked
  overnight or 2 x 14¹/₂ ounce cans
  lima beans
1 tbsp olive oil

2 garlic cloves, crushed
1 vegetable or chicken stock cube,
  crumbled
²/₃ cup milk

2 tbsp chopped fresh oregano
salt and pepper

1 If you are using dried beans that have been soaked overnight, drain them thoroughly. Bring a large pan of water to a boil, add the beans, and boil for 10 minutes. Cover the pan and simmer for a further 30 minutes or until tender. Drain the beans, reserving the cooking liquid. If you are using canned beans, drain them thoroughly and reserve the liquid.

2 Heat the oil in a large skillet and sauté the garlic for 2–3 minutes or until just beginning to brown.

3 Add the beans and 1²/₃ cups of the reserved liquid to the skillet, stirring constantly. You may need to add a little water if there is insufficient liquid. Stir in the crumbled stock cube. Bring the mixture to a boil, stirring, and then remove the skillet from the heat.

4 Place the bean mixture in a food processor and blend to form a smooth purée. Alternatively, mash the bean mixture to a smooth consistency. Season to taste with salt and pepper, and stir in the milk.

5 Pour the soup back into the skillet and gently heat to just below boiling point. Stir in the chopped oregano just before serving.

VARIATION

If you prefer, use 3 teaspoons of dried oregano instead of fresh, but add with the beans in step 2. This soup can also be made with cannellini or borlotti beans following the same method.

Brown Lentil Soup with Pasta

In Italy, this soup is called Minestrade Lentiche. *A minestra is a soup cooked with pasta; in this case farfalline, a small bow-shaped variety, is used. This hearty soup is a meal in itself.*

Serves 4

INGREDIENTS

4 slices bacon, cut into small squares
1 onion, chopped
2 garlic cloves, crushed

2 celery stalks, chopped
1/4 cup farfalline or spaghetti broken into small pieces
14 1/2 ounce can brown lentils, drained

5 cups hot ham or vegetable stock
2 tbsp chopped, fresh mint

1 Place the bacon in a large skillet together with the onions, garlic, and celery. Dry fry for 4–5 minutes, stirring, until the onion is tender and the bacon is just beginning to brown.

2 Add the farfalline or spaghetti pieces to the skillet and cook, stirring, for about 1 minute to coat the pasta in the oil.

3 Add the lentils and the stock and bring to a boil. Reduce the heat and simmer for 12–15 minutes or until the pasta is tender.

4 Remove the skillet from the heat and stir in the chopped fresh mint.

5 Transfer the soup to warm soup bowls and serve immediately.

COOK'S TIP

If you prefer to use dried lentils, add the stock before the pasta and cook for 1–1 1/4 hours, until the lentils are tender. Add the pasta and cook for a further 12–15 minutes.

VARIATION

Any type of pasta can be used in this recipe. Try fusilli, conchiglie, or rigatoni, if you prefer.

Vegetable Soup with Cannellini Beans

*This wonderful combination of beans, vegetables, and vermicelli is
made even richer by the addition of pesto and dried mushrooms.*

Serves 4

INGREDIENTS

1 small eggplant
2 large tomatoes
1 potato, peeled
1 carrot, peeled
1 leek
14$^{1}/_{2}$ ounce can cannellini beans

3$^{3}/_{4}$ cups hot vegetable or chicken
stock
2 tsp dried basil
$^{1}/_{2}$ ounce dried porcini mushrooms,
soaked for 10 minutes in enough
warm water to cover

$^{1}/_{4}$ cup vermicelli
3 tbsp pesto (see page 110 or use
ready-made)
freshly grated Parmesan cheese, to
serve (optional)

1 Using a sharp knife, slice
the eggplant into rings about
$^{1}/_{2}$ inch thick, then cut each ring
into 4.

2 Cut the tomatoes and
potato into small dice.
Cut the carrot into sticks, about
1 inch long and cut the leek
into rings.

3 Place the cannellini beans
and their liquid in a large
saucepan. Add the eggplant,
tomatoes, potatoes, carrot, and
leek, stirring to mix.

4 Add the stock to the pan and
bring to a boil. Reduce the
heat and simmer for 15 minutes.

5 Add the basil, dried
mushrooms, their soaking
liquid, and the vermicelli and
simmer for 5 minutes or until all
the vegetables are tender.

6 Remove the pan from the
heat and stir in the pesto.

7 Ladle into warm bowls and
serve with freshly grated
Parmesan cheese, if using.

COOK'S TIP

*Porcini
mushrooms are
grown in southern
Italy. When dried and
rehydrated they have a very intense
flavor, so although they are
expensive to buy, only a small
amount is required to add flavor to
soups or risottos.*

Creamy Tomato Soup

This quick and easy creamy soup has a lovely fresh tomato flavor.

Serves 4

INGREDIENTS

3 tbsp butter
1 pound 9 ounces ripe tomatoes,
   preferably plum, roughly chopped

$3^3/_4$ cups hot vegetable stock
$^2/_3$ cup milk or light cream
$^1/_4$ cup ground almonds
1 tsp sugar

2 tbsp shredded basil leaves
salt and pepper

1 Melt the butter in a large saucepan. Add the tomatoes and cook for 5 minutes, until the skins start to wrinkle. Season to taste with salt and pepper.

2 Add the stock to the pan, bring to a boil, cover, and simmer for 10 minutes.

3 Meanwhile, under a preheated broiler, lightly toast the ground almonds until they are golden brown. This will take only 1-2 minutes, so watch them closely.

4 Remove the soup from the heat, place in a food processor, and blend the mixture to form a smooth consistency. Alternatively, mash the soup with a potato masher.

5 Pass the soup through a strainer to remove any tomato skin or seeds.

6 Place the soup in the pan and return to the heat. Stir in the milk or cream, ground almonds, and sugar. Warm the soup through and add the shredded basil just before serving.

7 Transfer the creamy tomato soup to warm soup bowls and serve hot.

VARIATION

Very fine breadcrumbs can be used instead of the ground almonds, if desired. Toast them in the same way as the almonds and add with the milk or cream in step 6.

Tuscan Onion Soup

This soup is best made with white onions, which have a milder flavor than the more usual brown variety. If you cannot get ahold of them, try using large Spanish onions instead.

Serves 4

INGREDIENTS

$1/3$ cup diced pancetta
1 tbsp olive oil
4 large white onions, thinly sliced
   in rings
3 garlic cloves, chopped

$3^3/4$ cups hot chicken or ham stock
4 slices ciabatta or other
   Italian bread
3 tbsp butter

$2^3/4$ ounces Swiss or cheddar cheese
salt and pepper

1 Dry fry the pancetta in a large saucepan for 3–4 minutes, until it just begins to brown. Remove the pancetta from the saucepan and set aside until required.

2 Add the oil to the pan and sauté the onions and garlic over a high heat for 4 minutes. Reduce the heat, cover, and cook for 15 minutes, until lightly caramelized.

3 Add the stock to the saucepan and bring to a boil. Reduce the heat and simmer, covered, for about 10 minutes.

4 Toast the slices of ciabatta on both sides, under a preheated broiler, for 2–3 minutes, or until golden. Spread the ciabatta with butter and top with the Swiss or cheddar cheese. Cut the bread into bite-size pieces.

5 Add the reserved pancetta to the soup and season to taste with salt and pepper. Pour into 4 soup bowls and top with the toasted bread.

COOK'S TIP

Pancetta is similar to bacon, but it is air- and salt-cured for about 6 months. Pancetta is available from most delicatessens and some large supermarkets. If you cannot obtain pancetta, use unsmoked bacon instead.

Green Soup

*This fresh-tasting soup with green beans, cucumber, and watercress
can be served warm, or chilled on a hot summer day.*

Serves 4

INGREDIENTS

1 tbsp olive oil
1 onion, chopped
1 garlic clove, chopped
7 ounces potatoes, peeled and cut
   into 1-inch cubes

3 cups vegetable or chicken stock
1 small cucumber or $^{1}/_{2}$ large
   cucumber, cut into chunks

3 ounce bunch watercress
$4^{1}/_{2}$ ounces green beans, trimmed
   and halved lengthwise
salt and pepper

1 Heat the oil in a large pan
and sauté the onion and garlic
for 3–4 minutes, or until softened.
Add the cubed potatoes and cook
for a further 2–3 minutes.

2 Stir in the stock, bring to
a boil, and simmer for
5 minutes.

3 Add the cucumber to the
pan and cook for a further
3 minutes, or until the potatoes are
tender. Test by inserting the tip of
a knife into the potato cubes—it
should pass through easily.

4 Add the watercress and allow
to wilt. Then place the soup
in a food processor and blend until
smooth. Alternatively, before
adding the watercress, mash the
soup with a potato masher and
push through a strainer, then chop
the watercress finely and stir into
the soup.

5 Bring a small pan of water to a
boil and steam the beans for
3–4 minutes, or until tender.

6 Add the beans to the soup,
season, and warm through.

VARIATION

*Try using $4^{1}/_{2}$ ounces snow peas
instead of the beans,
if you prefer.*

Artichoke Soup

This refreshing chilled soup is ideal for al fresco dining.

Serves 4

INGREDIENTS

1 tbsp olive oil
1 onion, chopped
1 garlic clove, crushed

2 x 14 ounce cans artichoke hearts,
  drained
2½ cups hot vegetable stock
⅔ cup light cream

2 tbsp fresh thyme, stalks removed
2 sun-dried tomatoes, cut into strips
crusty bread, to serve

1 Heat the oil in a large saucepan and sauté the chopped onion and crushed garlic until just softened.

2 Using a sharp knife, roughly chop the artichoke hearts. Add the artichoke pieces to the onion and garlic mixture in the pan. Pour in the hot vegetable stock, stirring.

3 Bring the mixture to a boil, then reduce the heat, and simmer, covered, for about 3 minutes.

4 Place the mixture into a food processor and blend until smooth. Alternatively, push the mixture through a strainer to remove any lumps.

5 Return the soup to the saucepan. Stir the light cream and fresh thyme into the soup, mixing well.

6 Transfer the soup to a large bowl, cover, cool, and chill in the refrigerator for about 3–4 hours.

7 Transfer the chilled soup to individual soup bowls and garnish with strips of sun-dried tomato. Serve with lots of fresh, crusty bread.

VARIATION

Try adding 2 tablespoons of dry vermouth, such as Martini, to the soup in step 5 if you wish.

Orange, Thyme, & Pumpkin Soup

This thick, creamy soup has a wonderful, warming golden color. It is flavored with orange and thyme.

Serves 4

INGREDIENTS

2 tbsp olive oil
2 medium onions, chopped
2 cloves garlic, chopped
7 cups diced pumpkin

6¼ cups boiling vegetable or
 chicken stock
finely grated rind and juice of
 1 orange

3 tbsp fresh thyme, stalks removed
²/₃ cup milk
salt and pepper
crusty bread, to serve

1 Heat the olive oil in a large saucepan. Add the onions to the pan and sauté for 3–4 minutes, or until softened. Add the garlic and pumpkin and cook for a further 2 minutes, stirring well.

2 Add the boiling vegetable or chicken stock, orange rind and juice, and 2 tablespoons of the thyme to the pan. Simmer, covered, for 20 minutes, or until the pumpkin is tender.

3 Place the mixture in a food processor and blend until smooth. Alternatively, mash the mixture with a potato masher until smooth. Season to taste with salt and pepper.

4 Return the soup to the saucepan and add the milk. Reheat the soup for 3–4 minutes, or until it is piping hot, but not boiling. Sprinkle with the remaining fresh thyme just before serving.

5 Divide the soup between 4 warm soup bowls and serve with lots of fresh crusty bread.

COOK'S TIP

Pumpkins are usually large vegetables. To make things a little easier, buy a piece weighing about 2 pounds. Alternatively, make double the quantity and freeze the soup for up to 3 months.

Minestrone

*Minestrone translates as "big soup" in Italian. It is made all over Italy,
but this version comes from Livorno, a port on the western coast.*

Serves 4

INGREDIENTS

1 tbsp olive oil
$2/3$ cup diced pancetta
2 medium onions, chopped
2 cloves garlic, crushed
1 potato, peeled and cut into
$1/2$-inch cubes
1 carrot, peeled and cut into chunks
1 leek, sliced into rings

$1/4$ green cabbage, shredded
1 celery stalk, chopped
1 pound can chopped tomatoes
7 ounce can small navy beans,
drained and rinsed
$2 1/2$ cups hot ham or chicken stock
diluted with $2 1/2$ cups
boiling water

bouquet garni (2 bay leaves, 2 sprigs
rosemary, and 2 sprigs thyme, tied
together)
salt and pepper
freshly grated Parmesan cheese,
to serve

1 Heat the oil in a large
saucepan. Add the diced
pancetta, chopped onions, and
garlic, and sauté for about
5 minutes, or until the onions are
soft and golden.

2 Add the prepared potato,
carrot, leek, cabbage, and
celery to the saucepan. Cook
for a further 2 minutes, stirring
frequently to coat all the
vegetables in the oil.

3 Add the tomatoes, small navy
beans, hot ham or chicken
stock, and bouquet garni to the
pan, stirring to mix. Lower the
heat and simmer the soup,
covered, for 15–20 minutes, or
until all the vegetables are
just tender.

4 Remove the bouquet garni,
season with salt and pepper
to taste, and serve with plenty of
freshly grated Parmesan.

VARIATION

*Any combination of vegetables
will work equally well in this soup.
For a special minestrone, try adding
$1/2$ cup shredded prosciutto in
step 1.*

Calabrian Mushroom Soup

The Calabrian Mountains in southern Italy provide large amounts of exotic mushrooms.
They are rich in flavor and color and make a wonderful soup.

Serves 4

INGREDIENTS

2 tbsp olive oil
1 onion, chopped
1 pound mixed mushrooms, such as
   ceps, oyster, and button

1¹/₄ cups milk
3³/₄ cups hot vegetable stock
8 slices of rustic bread or French
   bread
3 tbsp butter, melted

2 garlic cloves, crushed
³/₄ cup finely grated Swiss cheese
salt and pepper

1 Heat the oil in a large skillet and sauté the onion for 3–4 minutes, or until soft and golden.

2 Wipe each mushroom with a damp cloth and cut any large mushrooms into smaller, bite-size pieces.

3 Add the mushrooms to the pan, stirring quickly to coat them in the oil.

4 Add the milk to the pan, bring to a boil, cover, lower the heat, and simmer for about 5 minutes. Gradually stir in the hot vegetable stock.

5 Under a preheated broiler, toast the bread on both sides until golden.

6 Mix together the garlic and butter and spoon generously over the toast.

7 Place the toast in the bottom of a large tureen or divide it between 4 individual serving bowls and pour in the hot soup. Top with the grated Swiss cheese and serve at once.

COOK'S TIP

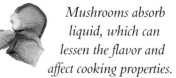

Mushrooms absorb liquid, which can lessen the flavor and affect cooking properties. Wipe them with a damp cloth rather than rinsing them in water.

VARIATION

Supermarkets stock a wide variety of exotic mushrooms. If you prefer, use a combination of cultivated and exotic mushrooms.

Tomatoes Stuffed with Tuna Mayonnaise

*Deliciously sweet roasted tomatoes are filled with
homemade lemon mayonnaise and tuna.*

Serves 4

INGREDIENTS

4 plum tomatoes
2 tbsp sun-dried tomato paste
2 egg yolks
2 tsp lemon juice
finely grated rind of 1 lemon

4 tbsp olive oil
4 ounce can tuna, drained
2 tbsp capers, rinsed
salt and pepper

TO GARNISH:
2 sun-dried tomatoes, cut into strips
fresh basil leaves

1 Halve the tomatoes and scoop out the seeds. Divide the sun-dried tomato paste among the tomato halves and spread around the inside of the skin.

2 Place on a cookie sheet and roast in a preheated oven at 400°F for 12–15 minutes. Cool slightly.

3 Meanwhile, make the mayonnaise. In a food processor, blend the egg yolks and lemon juice with the lemon rind until smooth. Once mixed and with the motor still running, slowly add the olive oil. Stop the processor as soon as the mayonnaise has thickened. Alternatively, use a hand whisk, beating the mixture continuously until it thickens.

4 Add the tuna and capers to the mayonnaise and season with salt and pepper to taste.

5 Spoon the tuna mayonnaise mixture into the tomato shells and garnish with sun-dried tomato strips and basil leaves. Return to the oven for a few minutes or serve chilled.

COOK'S TIP

For a picnic, do not roast the tomatoes, just scoop out the seeds, drain, cut-side down, on absorbent paper towels for 1 hour, and fill with the mayonnaise mixture. They are firmer to handle and easier to eat with the fingers this way. If you prefer, ready-made mayonnaise may be used instead—just stir in the lemon rind.

Deep-fried Risotto Balls

The Italian name for this dish translates as "telephone wires," which refers to the strings of melted mozzarella cheese, the surprise contained within the risotto balls.

Serves 4

INGREDIENTS

2 tbsp olive oil
1 medium onion, finely chopped
1 garlic clove, chopped
$^1/_2$ red bell pepper, diced

$^3/_4$ cup risotto rice, washed
1 tsp dried oregano
$1^2/_3$ cup hot vegetable or chicken
  stock

$^1/_2$ cup dry white wine
$2^3/_4$ ounces mozzarella cheese
oil, for deep-frying
fresh basil sprig, to garnish

1 Heat the oil in a skillet and sauté the onion and garlic for 3–4 minutes, or until just softened.

2 Add the bell pepper, rice, and oregano to the pan. Cook for 2–3 minutes, stirring to coat the rice in the oil.

3 Mix the stock together with the wine and add to the pan a ladleful at a time, waiting for the liquid to be absorbed by the rice before you add the next ladleful of liquid.

4 Once all the liquid has been absorbed and the rice is tender (about 15 minutes total), remove the pan from the heat and leave until the mixture is cool enough to handle.

5 Cut the cheese into 12 pieces. Taking about a tablespoon of risotto, shape the mixture around the cheese pieces to make 12 balls.

6 Heat the oil until a piece of bread browns in 30 seconds. Cook the risotto balls in batches of 4 for 2 minutes, until golden.

7 Remove the risotto balls with a slotted spoon and drain thoroughly on absorbent paper towels. Garnish with a sprig of basil and serve hot.

VARIATION

Although mozzarella is the traditional cheese for this recipe and creates the stringy "telephone wire" effect, other cheeses, such as cheddar, may be used if desired.

Black Olive Pâté

*The flavor of olives is accentuated by the anchovies, and the pâté is
wonderful served as an appetizer on thin pieces of toast with a very dry white wine.*

Serves 4

INGREDIENTS

1¹/2 cups pitted black olives, chopped
finely grated rind and juice of
   1 lemon
3 tbsp sweet butter

4 canned anchovy fillets, drained and
rinsed

2 tbsp extra-virgin olive oil
2 tbsp ground almonds

1 If you are making the pâté
by hand, chop the olives very
finely and then mash them,
together with the lemon rind,
juice, and butter, using a fork or
potato masher. Alternatively, place
the olives, lemon rind, juice, and
butter in a food processor and
blend until all the ingredients are
finely chopped.

2 Using a sharp knife, chop
the drained anchovies and
add them to the olive and lemon
mixture. Mash the pâté by hand
or blend it in a food processor
for about 20 seconds.

3 Gradually beat in the olive oil
and stir in the ground
almonds. Place the black olive
pâté in a serving bowl.

4 Chill the pâté in the
refrigerator for about
30 minutes. Serve accompanied
by thin pieces of toast.

COOK'S TIP

*Extra-virgin olive oil is the finest
grade of olive oil. It is made from
the first, cold pressing of hand
gathered olives.*

COOK'S TIP

*The pâté will keep for up to
5 days in a serving bowl in the
refrigerator if you pour a thin layer
of extra-virgin olive oil over the top
to seal it. Then use the oil to brush
on the toast before spreading
the pâté.*

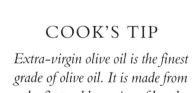

Fresh Figs with Prosciutto

This colorful fresh salad is delicious at any time of the year.

Serves 4

INGREDIENTS

1¹/₂ ounces arugula
4 fresh figs
4 slices prosciutto

4 tbsp olive oil
1 tbsp fresh orange juice

1 tbsp clear honey
1 small red chili

1 Tear the arugula into fairly small pieces and arrange on 4 serving plates.

2 Using a sharp knife, cut each of the figs into quarters and place them on top of the arugula leaves.

3 Using a sharp knife, cut the prosciutto into strips and scatter over the arugula and figs.

4 Place the oil, orange juice, and honey in a screw-top jar. Shake the jar vigorously until the mixture emulsifies and forms a thick dressing. Transfer to a serving bowl.

5 Using a sharp knife, dice the chili, remembering not to touch your face before you have washed your hands (see Cook's Tip, right). Add the chopped chili to the dressing and mix well.

6 Drizzle the dressing over the prosciutto, arugula, and figs, tossing to mix well. Serve the salad at once.

COOK'S TIP

Parma, in the Emilia-Romagna region of Italy, is famous for its ham, prosciutto di Parma, thought to be the best in the world.

COOK'S TIP

Chilies can burn the skin for several hours after chopping, so it is advisable to wear gloves when you are handling the very hot varieties.

Roasted Bell Peppers

*These bell peppers can be used as an antipasto, as a side
dish, or as a relish to accompany meat and fish.*

Serves 4

INGREDIENTS

2 each, red, yellow, and orange bell
peppers
4 tomatoes, halved

1 tbsp olive oil
3 garlic cloves, chopped
1 onion, sliced in rings

2 tbsp fresh thyme
salt and pepper

1 Halve and seed the bell
peppers. Place them, cut-side
down, on a cookie sheet and cook
under a preheated broiler for
10 minutes.

2 Add the tomatoes to the
cookie sheet and broil for
5 minutes, until the skins of the
bell peppers and tomatoes are
charred.

3 Put the bell peppers into a
plastic bag for 10 minutes to
sweat, which will make the skin
easier to peel. Remove the tomato
skins and roughly chop the flesh.

4 Peel the skins from the bell
peppers and slice the flesh
into strips.

5 Heat the oil in a large skillet
and sauté the garlic and onion
for 3–4 minutes, or until softened.

6 Add the bell peppers and
tomatoes to the skillet and
cook for 5 minutes. Stir in the
fresh thyme and season to taste
with salt and pepper.

7 Transfer to serving bowls and
serve warm. Alternatively,
chill before serving.

COOK'S TIP

*You can preserve
the bell peppers in
the refrigerator by
placing them in a
sterilized jar and pouring olive oil
over the top to seal. Alternatively,
heat ¼ cup white wine vinegar
with a bay leaf and
4 juniper berries and bring to a
boiling point. Pour over the bell
peppers and set aside until
completely cold. Pack into sterilized
jars—they will keep for up
to one month.*

Baked Eggplant & Tomatoes

This dish is a bit like an eggplant lasagne with layers of eggplant, tomato sauce, and mozzarella combining with Parmesan cheese to create a wonderfully tasty starter.

Serves 4

INGREDIENTS

3–4 tbsp olive oil
2 garlic cloves, crushed
2 large eggplant

$3^1/_2$ ounces mozzarella cheese,
  thinly sliced
7 ounces tomato sauce

$^2/_3$ cup grated Parmesan cheese

1 Heat 2 tablespoons of the olive oil in a large skillet. Add the garlic to the skillet and sauté for 30 seconds.

2 Slice the eggplant lengthwise. Add the slices to the skillet and cook them in the oil for about 3–4 minutes on each side, or until just tender. (You will probably have to cook them in batches, so add the remaining olive oil as necessary.)

3 Remove the eggplant slices with a slotted spoon and drain thoroughly on absorbent paper towels.

4 Place a layer of eggplant slices in a shallow ovenproof dish. Cover the eggplant with a layer of mozzarella cheese and then pour a third of the tomato sauce on top. Continue layering in the same order, finishing with a layer of tomato sauce on top.

5 Generously sprinkle the grated Parmesan cheese over the top and then bake in a preheated oven at 400°F for 25–30 minutes.

6 Transfer the baked eggplant and tomatoes to serving plates and serve warm or chilled.

COOK'S TIP

Passata is a simple tomato sauce, which can be bought from most supermarkets. Alternatively, you can purée and sieve a can of tomatoes and season with salt and pepper to taste.

Zucchini & Thyme Fritters

*These tasty little fritters are great with roasted bell peppers
(see page 36) as hors d'oeuvres for a cocktail party.*

Makes: 16 medium fritters or about 30 small fritters

INGREDIENTS

$^3/_4$ cup self–rising flour
2 eggs, beaten
$^1/_4$ cup milk

10 $^1/_2$ ounces zucchini
2 tbsp fresh thyme

1 tbsp oil
salt and pepper

1 Sift the self-rising flour into a large bowl and make a well in the center. Add the eggs to the well, and using a wooden spoon, gradually fold in the flour.

2 Slowly add the milk to the mixture, stirring constantly to form a thick batter.

3 Wash the zucchini. Grate the zucchini over a paper towel placed in a bowl to absorb some of the juices.

4 Add the zucchini, thyme, and salt and pepper to taste to the batter, and mix thoroughly.

5 Heat the oil in a large, heavy-based skillet. Taking a tablespoon of the batter for a medium-size fritter or half a tablespoon of batter for a smaller-size fritter, spoon the mixture into the hot oil and cook, in batches, for 3–4 minutes on each side.

6 Remove the fritters with a slotted spoon and drain thoroughly on absorbent paper towels. Keep each batch of fritters warm in the oven while making the rest. Serve hot.

VARIATION

Try adding $^1/_2$ teaspoon dried, crushed chilies in step 4 for spicier tasting fritters.

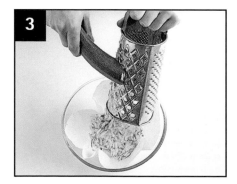

Cured Meats with Olives &Tomatoes

This is a typical antipasto dish with the cold cured meats, stuffed olives, fresh tomatoes, basil, and balsamic vinegar.

Serves 4

INGREDIENTS

4 plum tomatoes
1 tbsp balsamic vinegar
6 canned anchovy fillets, drained
   and rinsed

2 tbsp capers, drained and rinsed
1 cup pitted green olives
6 ounces mixed, cured meats, sliced
8 fresh basil leaves

1 tbsp extra-virgin olive oil
salt and pepper
crusty bread, to serve

1 Using a sharp knife, cut the tomatoes into evenly sized slices. Sprinkle the tomato slices with the balsamic vinegar and a little salt and pepper to taste and set aside.

2 Chop the anchovy fillets into pieces measuring about the same length as the olives.

3 Push a piece of anchovy and a caper into each olive.

4 Arrange the sliced meat on 4 individual serving plates together with the tomatoes, filled olives, and basil leaves.

5 Lightly drizzle the olive oil over the sliced meat, tomatoes, and olives.

6 Serve the cured meats, olives, and tomatoes with lots of fresh crusty bread.

COOK'S TIP

The cured meats for this recipe are up to your individual taste. They can include a selection of prosciutto, pancetta, bresaola (dried salt beef), and salame di Milano (pork and beef sausage).

COOK'S TIP

Fill a screw-top jar with the stuffed olives, cover with olive oil, and use when required—they will keep for one month in the refrigerator.

Spinach & Ricotta Patties

"Nudo" or naked is the word used to describe this mixture, which can also be made into thin pancakes or used as a filling for tortellini.

Serves 4

INGREDIENTS

1 pound fresh spinach
1¹/₈ cups ricotta cheese
1 egg, beaten
2 tsp fennel seeds, lightly crushed

²/₃ cup finely grated pecorino or
  Parmesan cheese
¹/₄ cup all-purpose flour, mixed with
  1 tsp dried thyme
5 tbsp butter

2 garlic cloves, crushed
salt and pepper

1 Wash the spinach and trim off any long stalks. Place in a pan, cover, and cook for 4–5 minutes, until wilted. This will probably have to be done in batches as the volume of spinach is quite large. Place in a colander to drain, and cool.

2 Mash the ricotta and beat in the egg and the fennel seeds. Season with plenty of salt and pepper, then stir in the pecorino or Parmesan cheese.

3 Squeeze as much excess water as possible from the spinach and finely chop the leaves. Stir into the cheese mixture.

4 Taking about 1 tablespoon of the spinach and cheese mixture, shape it into a ball and flatten it slightly to form a patty. Gently roll in the seasoned flour. Continue this process until all the mixture has been used up.

5 Half fill a large saucepan with water and bring to a boil. Carefully add the patties and cook for 3–4 minutes, or until they rise to the surface. Remove with a slotted spoon.

6 Melt the butter in a pan. Add the garlic and sauté for 2–3 minutes. Pour the garlic butter over the patties, season with freshly ground black pepper, and serve at once.

COOK'S TIP

Once it is washed, spinach holds enough water on the leaves to cook without adding any extra liquid. If you use frozen spinach instead of fresh, simply thaw it and squeeze out the excess water.

Sweet & Sour Baby Onions

This is a typical Sicilian dish, combining honey and vinegar to give a delicate sweet and sour flavor. Serve hot as an accompaniment or cold with cured meats.

Serves 4

INGREDIENTS

12 ounces baby or pickling onions
2 tbsp olive oil
2 fresh bay leaves, torn into strips

thinly pared rind of 1 lemon
1 tbsp brown sugar
1 tbsp clear honey

4 tbsp red wine vinegar

1 Soak the onions in a bowl of boiling water—this will make them easier to peel. Using a sharp knife, peel and halve the onions.

2 Heat the oil in a large skillet. Add the bay leaves and onions to the pan and cook over a medium-high heat for 5–6 minutes, or until browned all over.

3 Cut the lemon rind into thin matchsticks. Add to the skillet with the sugar and honey. Cook for 2-3 minutes, stirring occasionally, until the onions are lightly caramelized.

4 Add the red wine vinegar to the skillet, being careful because it will spit. Cook for about 5 minutes, stirring, or until the onions are tender and the liquid has all but disappeared.

5 Transfer the onions to a serving dish and serve at once.

COOK'S TIP

Adjust the piquancy of this dish to your liking by adding more sugar for a sweeter, more caramelized taste, or extra red wine vinegar for a sharper, tarter flavor.

COOK'S TIP

To make the onions easier to peel, place them in a large saucepan, add boiling water, and set aside for 10 minutes. Drain the onions thoroughly, and when they are cold enough to handle, peel them.

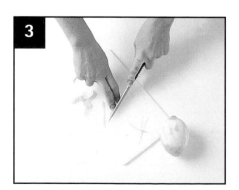

Stewed Artichokes

This is a traditional Roman dish. The artichokes are stewed in olive oil with fresh herbs.

Serves 4

INGREDIENTS

4 small globe artichokes
4 garlic cloves, peeled

2 bay leaves
finely grated rind and juice of
　1 lemon

olive oil
2 tbsp fresh marjoram
lemon wedges, to serve

1 Using a sharp knife, carefully peel away the tough outer leaves surrounding the artichokes. Trim the artichoke stems to about 1 inch.

2 Using a knife, cut each artichoke in half and scoop out the choke.

3 Place the artichokes in a large heavy-based pan. Add enough olive oil to half cover the artichokes in the pan.

4 Add the garlic cloves, bay leaves, and half of the grated lemon rind.

5 Start to heat the artichokes gently, cover the pan, and continue to cook over a low heat for about 40 minutes. The artichokes should be stewed in the oil, not fried.

6 Once the artichokes are tender, remove them with a slotted spoon and drain thoroughly. Remove the bay leaves.

7 Transfer the artichokes to warm serving plates. Serve the artichokes sprinkled with the remaining grated lemon rind, fresh marjoram, and a little lemon juice.

COOK'S TIP

To prevent the artichokes from oxidizing and turning brown before cooking, brush them with a little lemon juice. In addition, use the oil used for cooking the artichokes for salad dressings—it will impart a lovely lemon and herb flavor.

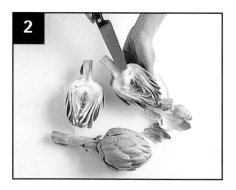

Garbanzo Beans with Prosciutto

Prosciutto is a cured ham, which is air- and salt-dried for up to one year. There are many different varieties available, and the one used here is crudo, which is slightly coarser than other types.

Serves 4

INGREDIENTS

1 tbsp olive oil
1 medium onion, thinly sliced
1 garlic clove, chopped

1 small red bell pepper, seeded and
  cut into thin strips
1¼ cups chopped prosciutto

14 ounce can garbanzo beans,
  drained and rinsed
1 tbsp chopped parsley, to garnish
crusty bread, to serve

1 Heat the oil in a large skillet. Add the sliced onion, chopped garlic, and sliced bell pepper and sauté for 3–4 minutes, or until the vegetables have softened.

2 Add the prosciutto to the skillet and fry with the vegetables for 5 minutes, or until the prosciutto is just beginning to brown.

3 Add the garbanzo beans to the skillet and cook, stirring, for 2–3 minutes, until warmed through.

4 Sprinkle with chopped parsley and transfer to warm serving plates. Serve with lots of fresh crusty bread.

COOK'S TIP

Whenever possible, use fresh herbs when cooking. They are becoming more readily available, especially since the introduction of "growing" herbs, small pots of herbs that you can buy from the supermarket and grow at home. This ensures the herbs are fresh and also provides a continuous supply.

VARIATION

Try adding a small finely diced chili in step 1 for a spicier taste, if desired.

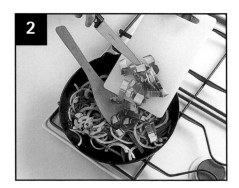

Deep-fried Seafood

Deep-fried seafood is popular all around the Mediterranean, where fish of all kinds is fresh and abundant. Serve with garlic mayonnaise and lemon wedges.

Serves 4

INGREDIENTS

7 ounces prepared squid
7 ounces raw tiger shrimp, peeled
5¹/₂ ounces whitebait
oil, for deep-frying

¹/₃ cup all-purpose flour
1 tsp dried basil
salt and pepper

TO SERVE:
garlic mayonnaise (see Cook's Tip)
lemon wedges

1 Carefully rinse the squid, shrimp, and whitebait under cold running water, in order to completely removing any dirt or grit.

2 Using a sharp knife, slice the squid into rings, leaving the tentacles whole.

3 Heat the oil in a large pan until a cube of bread browns in 30 seconds—the oil will then be hot enough for deep-frying.

4 Place the flour in a bowl and season with the salt, pepper, and basil.

5 Roll the squid, shrimp, and whitebait in the seasoned flour until coated all over. Carefully shake off any excess flour.

6 Cook the seafood in the hot oil in batches for 2–3 minutes, or until crispy and golden all over. Remove the seafood with a slotted spoon and drain thoroughly on paper towels. Keep warm while you cook the remaining batches.

7 Transfer the deep-fried seafood to serving plates and serve with garlic mayonnaise (see Cook's Tip) and lemon wedges.

COOK'S TIP

To make garlic mayonnaise for serving with the deep-fried seafood, crush 2 garlic cloves, stir into 8 tablespoons of mayonnaise, and season with salt and pepper and a little chopped parsley.

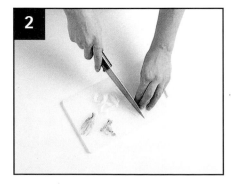

Tuscan Bean Salad with Tuna

The combination of beans and tuna is a favorite with the people of Tuscany. The hint of honey and lemon in the dressing makes this salad refreshing as well as hearty.

Serves 4

INGREDIENTS

1 small white onion or 2 scallions, finely chopped
2 x 14 ounce cans dried lima beans, drained

2 medium tomatoes
6¹/2 ounce can tuna, drained
2 tbsp flat leaf parsley, chopped
2 tbsp olive oil

1 tbsp lemon juice
2 tsp clear honey
1 garlic clove, crushed

1 Place the chopped onion or scallions and lima beans in a bowl and mix well to combine.

2 Using a sharp knife, cut the tomatoes into wedges. Add the tomatoes to the onion and bean mixture.

3 Flake the tuna with a fork and add it to the onion and bean mixture, together with the parsley.

4 In a screw-top jar, mix together the olive oil, lemon juice, honey, and garlic. Shake the jar vigorously until the dressing emulsifies and thickens.

5 Pour the dressing over the bean salad. Toss the ingredients together using 2 spoons and serve.

COOK'S TIP

This salad will keep for several days in a covered container in the refrigerator. Make up the dressing just before serving and toss the ingredients together to mix well.

VARIATION

Substitute fresh salmon for the tuna if you wish to create a luxurious version of this recipe for a special occasion.

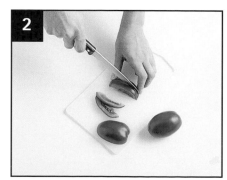

Italian Potato Salad

Potato salad is always a favorite, but it is even more delicious with the addition of sun-dried tomatoes and fresh parsley.

Serves 4

INGREDIENTS

1 pound baby potatoes, unpeeled, or larger potatoes, halved
4 tbsp unsweetened yogurt

4 tbsp mayonnaise
8 sun-dried tomatoes

2 tbsp flat leaf parsley, chopped
salt and pepper

1 Rinse and clean the potatoes and place them in a large pan of water. Bring to a boil and cook for 8–12 minutes, or until just tender. (The cooking time will vary according to the size of your potatoes.)

2 Using a sharp knife, cut the sun-dried tomatoes into thin slices.

3 To make the dressing, mix together the yogurt and mayonnaise in a bowl and season to taste with a little salt and pepper. Stir in the sun-dried tomato slices and the chopped flat leaf parsley.

4 Remove the potatoes with a slotted spoon, drain them thoroughly, and then set them aside to cool. If you are using larger potatoes, cut them into 2-inch chunks.

5 Pour the dressing over the potatoes and toss to mix.

6 Chill the potato salad in the refrigerator for about 20 minutes, then serve as a starter or as an accompaniment.

COOK'S TIP

It is easier to cut the larger potatoes once they are cooked. Although smaller pieces of potato will cook more quickly, they tend to disintegrate and become mushy.

Green Salad

This is a green salad with a difference—herb-flavored croûtons are topped with peppery arugula, red chard, green olives, and pistachios to make an elegant combination.

Serves 4

INGREDIENTS

¹⁄₄ cup pistachios	1 tbsp red wine vinegar	¹⁄₂ cup pitted green olives
5 tbsp extra-virgin olive oil	1 tsp wholegrain mustard	2 tbsp fresh basil, shredded
1 tbsp rosemary, chopped	1 tsp sugar	
2 garlic cloves, chopped	1 ounce arugula	
4 slices rustic bread	1 ounce red chard	

1 Shell the pistachios and roughly chop them, using a sharp knife.

2 Heat 2 tablespoons of the extra-virgin olive oil in a skillet. Add the rosemary and garlic and cook over a medium heat for 2 minutes.

3 Add the slices of bread to the skillet and fry for 2–3 minutes on both sides, until golden. Remove the bread from the pan and drain on absorbent paper towels.

4 To make the dressing, mix together the remaining olive oil, the red wine vinegar, mustard, and sugar.

5 Place a slice of bread onto 4 serving plates and top with the arugula and red chard. Sprinkle with the olives.

6 Drizzle the dressing over the top of the salad greens. Sprinkle with the chopped pistachios and shredded basil leaves and serve the salad immediately.

COOK'S TIP

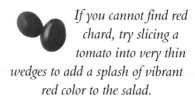

If you cannot find red chard, try slicing a tomato into very thin wedges to add a splash of vibrant red color to the salad.

VARIATION

Watercress may be used instead of the arugula, if desired.

Minted Fennel Salad

This is a very refreshing salad. The subtle licorice flavor of fennel combines well with the cucumber and mint.

Serves 4

INGREDIENTS

1 bulb fennel
2 small oranges

1 small or $^1/_2$ a large cucumber
1 tbsp chopped mint

1 tbsp virgin olive oil
2 eggs, hard-boiled

1 Using a sharp knife, trim the outer leaves from the fennel bulb. Slice the fennel bulb thinly into a bowl of water and sprinkle with lemon juice (see Cook's Tip).

2 Grate the rind of the oranges over a bowl. Using a sharp knife, pare away the orange pith, then segment the oranges by carefully slicing between each line of pith. Do this over the bowl in order to retain the juice.

3 Using a sharp knife, cut the cucumber into $^1/_2$-inch slices and then cut each slice into quarters. Add the cucumber to the fennel and orange mixture together with the mint.

4 Pour the olive oil over the fennel and cucumber salad and toss well.

5 Peel and quarter the eggs and use them to decorate the top of the salad. Serve at once.

COOK'S TIP

Virgin olive oil, which has a fine aroma and flavor, is made by the cold pressing of olives. However, it may have a slightly higher acidity level than extra-virgin oil.

COOK'S TIP

Fennel will discolor if it is left for any length of time without a dressing. To prevent any discoloration, place it in a bowl of water and sprinkle with lemon juice.

Capri Salad

This tomato, olive, and mozzarella salad, dressed with balsamic vinegar and olive oil, makes a delicious starter on its own. Increase the quantity by half to make a full salad for four people.

Serves 4

INGREDIENTS

2 beef tomatoes
$4^1/_2$ ounces mozzarella cheese
12 black olives

8 basil leaves
1 tbsp balsamic vinegar
1 tbsp olive oil

salt and pepper
basil leaves, to garnish

1 Using a sharp knife, cut the tomatoes into thin slices.

2 Using a sharp knife, cut the mozzarella into slices.

3 Pit the olives and slice them into rings.

4 Layer the tomato, mozzarella cheese, and olives in a stack, finishing with a layer of cheese on top.

5 Place each stack under a preheated hot broiler for 2–3 minutes, or just long enough to melt the mozzarella.

6 Drizzle with the vinegar and olive oil, and season to taste with salt and pepper.

7 Transfer to serving plates and garnish with basil leaves. Serve immediately.

COOK'S TIP

Buffalo mozzarella cheese, although it is usually more expensive because of the comparative rarity of buffalo, does have a better flavor than the cow's milk variety. It is popular in salads, but also provides a tangy layer in baked dishes.

COOK'S TIP

Balsamic vinegar, which has grown in popularity over the past decade, is produced in the Emilia-Romagna region of Italy. It is made from wine that is distilled until it is dark brown and extremely strongly flavored.

Mushroom Salad

Raw mushrooms are a great favorite in Italian dishes—
they have a fresh, almost creamy flavor.

Serves 4

INGREDIENTS

5¹/₂ ounces firm white mushrooms
4 tbsp virgin olive oil

1 tbsp lemon juice
5 anchovy fillets, drained and
chopped

1 tbsp fresh marjoram
salt and pepper

1 Gently wipe each mushroom with a damp cloth to remove any excess dirt. Slice the mushrooms thinly, using a sharp knife.

2 Mix together the olive oil and lemon juice and pour the mixture over the mushrooms. Toss together so that the mushrooms are completely coated with the lemon juice and oil.

3 Stir the chopped anchovy fillets into the mushrooms. Season the mushroom mixture with black pepper and garnish with the fresh marjoram.

4 Let the mushroom salad stand for 5 minutes before serving in order for all the flavors to be absorbed. Season with a little salt (see Cook's Tip, below) and then serve.

COOK'S TIP

Do not season the mushroom salad with salt until the very last minute as it will cause the mushrooms to blacken and the juices to leak. The result will not be as tasty as it should be as the full flavors won't be absorbed and it will also look very unattractive.

COOK'S TIP

If you use dried herbs rather than fresh, remember that you need only about one-third of dried to fresh.

Yellow Bell Pepper Salad

A colorful combination of yellow bell peppers, red radishes, and celery combine to give a wonderfully crunchy texture and fresh taste.

Serves 4

INGREDIENTS

4 slices bacon, chopped
2 yellow bell peppers
8 radishes, washed and trimmed

1 celery stalk, finely chopped
3 plum tomatoes, cut into wedges
3 tbsp olive oil

1 tbsp fresh thyme

1 Dry fry the chopped bacon in a skillet for 4–5 minutes, or until crispy. Remove the bacon from the skillet, set aside, and cool until required.

2 Using a sharp knife, halve and seed the bell peppers. Slice the bell peppers into long strips.

3 Using a sharp knife, halve the radishes and cut them into wedges.

4 Mix together the bell peppers, radishes, celery, and tomatoes, and toss the mixture in the olive oil and fresh thyme. Season to taste with a little salt and pepper.

5 Transfer the salad to serving plates and garnish with the reserved crispy bacon.

COOK'S TIP

Tomatoes are actually berries and are related to potatoes. There are many different shapes and sizes of this versatile fruit. The one most used in Italian cooking is the plum tomato, which is very flavorsome.

COOK'S TIP

Pre-packaged diced bacon can be purchased from most supermarkets, which helps to save on preparation time.

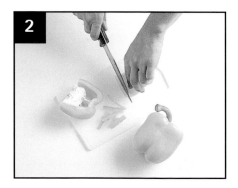

Spinach Salad

Fresh baby spinach is tasty and light, and it makes an excellent salad to go with the chicken and creamy dressing.

Serves 4

INGREDIENTS

1³/₄ ounces mushrooms
3¹/₂ ounces baby spinach, washed
2³/₄ ounces radicchio leaves,
    shredded

3¹/₂ ounces cooked chicken,
    preferably breast
1³/₄ ounces prosciutto
2 tbsp olive oil

finely grated rind of ¹/₂ orange and
    juice of 1 orange
1 tbsp unsweetened yogurt

1 Wipe the mushrooms with a damp cloth to remove any excess dirt.

2 Gently mix together the spinach and radicchio in a large salad bowl.

3 Thinly slice the wiped mushrooms and add them to the bowl containing the spinach and radicchio.

4 Tear the cooked chicken breast and prosciutto into strips and mix them into the salad.

5 To make the dressing, place the olive oil, orange rind, juice, and yogurt into a screw-top jar. Shake the jar until the mixture is well combined. Season to taste with salt and pepper.

6 Drizzle the dressing over the spinach salad and toss to mix well. Serve immediately.

COOK'S TIP

Radiccio is a variety of endive originating in Italy. It has a slightly bitter flavor.

VARIATION

Spinach is delicious when served raw. Try raw spinach in a salad garnished with bacon or garlicky croûtons. The young leaves have a wonderfully sharp flavor.

Sweet & Sour Eggplant Salad

This cooked salad from Sicily was first brought to Italy by the Moors.

Serves 4

INGREDIENTS

6 tbsp olive oil
1 onion, chopped
2 garlic cloves, chopped
2 celery stalks, chopped
1 pound eggplant

14 ounce can tomatoes, chopped
$^{1}/_{2}$ cup pitted green olives, chopped
2 tbsp sugar

$2^{1}/_{3}$ cup red wine vinegar
1 ounce capers, drained
salt and pepper
1 tbsp flat leaf parsley, roughly
    chopped, to garnish

1 Heat 2 tablespoons of the oil in a large skillet. Add the prepared onions, garlic, and celery to the skillet and cook, stirring, for 3–4 minutes.

2 Using a sharp knife, slice the eggplant into thick rounds, then cut each round into 4 pieces.

3 Add the eggplant pieces to the skillet with the remaining olive oil and fry for 5 minutes, or until golden.

4 Add the tomatoes, olives, and sugar to the skillet, stirring until the sugar has completely dissolved.

5 Add the red wine vinegar, reduce the heat, and simmer for 10–15 minutes or until the sauce is thick and the eggplant slices are tender.

6 While the skillet is still on the heat, carefully stir in the capers. Season to taste with a little salt and pepper.

7 Transfer to serving plates and garnish with the chopped fresh parsley.

COOK'S TIP

This salad is best served cold the day after it is made, which allows the flavors to mingle and be fully absorbed.

Lentil & Tuna Salad

In this recipe, lentils, combined with spices, lemon juice, and tuna, make a wonderfully tasty and filling salad.

Serves 4

INGREDIENTS

3 tbsp virgin olive oil
1 tbsp lemon juice
1 tsp wholegrain mustard
1 garlic clove, crushed

$^1/_2$ tsp ground cumin
$^1/_2$ tsp ground coriander
1 small red onion
2 ripe tomatoes
14 ounce can lentils, drained

6$^1/_2$ can tuna, drained
2 tbsp fresh cilantro, chopped
pepper

1 Using a sharp knife, seed and dice the tomatoes.

2 Using a sharp knife, finely chop the red onion.

3 To make the dressing, beat together the virgin olive oil, lemon juice, mustard, garlic, ground cumin, and ground coriander in a small bowl. Set aside until required.

4 Carefully mix together the chopped onion, diced tomatoes, and drained lentils in a large bowl.

5 Flake the tuna and stir it into the onion, tomato, and lentil mixture.

6 Stir in the chopped fresh cilantro.

7 Pour the dressing over the lentil and tuna salad and season with freshly ground black pepper. Serve at once.

VARIATION

Nuts would add extra flavor and texture to this salad.

COOK'S TIP

Lentils are a good source of protein and contain important vitamins and minerals. Buy them dried for soaking and cooking yourself, or buy canned varieties for speed and convenience.

Bruschetta with Tomatoes

*Using ripe tomatoes and the best olive oil will
make this Tuscan dish absolutely delicious.*

Serves 4

INGREDIENTS

10 1/2 ounces cherry tomatoes
4 sun-dried tomatoes
4 tbsp extra-virgin olive oil

16 fresh basil leaves, shredded
2 garlic cloves, peeled
8 slices ciabatta

salt and pepper

1 Using a sharp knife, cut the cherry tomatoes in half.

2 Using a sharp knife, slice the sun-dried tomatoes into strips.

3 Place the cherry tomatoes and sun-dried tomatoes in a bowl. Add the olive oil and the shredded basil leaves and toss to mix well. Season to taste with a little salt and pepper.

4 Using a sharp knife, cut the garlic cloves in half. Lightly toast the ciabatta bread.

5 Rub the garlic, cut-side down, over both sides of the toasted ciabatta bread.

6 Top the ciabatta bread with the tomato mixture and serve immediately.

COOK'S TIP

*Ciabatta is an Italian rustic
bread which is slightly holed
and quite chewy. It is very good
in this recipe as it absorbs the
full flavor of the garlic and
extra-virgin olive oil.*

VARIATION

*Plum tomatoes are also
good in this recipe.
Halve them, then cut
them into wedges. Mix them with
the sun-dried tomatoes in step 3.*

Italian Omelet

A baked omelet of substantial proportions with potatoes, onions, artichokes, and sun-dried tomatoes.

Serves 4

INGREDIENTS

2 pounds potatoes
1 tbsp oil
1 large onion, sliced
2 garlic cloves, chopped

6 sun-dried tomatoes, cut into strips
14 ounce can artichoke hearts,
 drained and halved
$1^1/_8$ cups ricotta cheese

4 large eggs, beaten
2 tbsp milk
$^2/_3$ cup grated Parmesan cheese
3 tbsp chopped thyme

1 Peel the potatoes and place them in a bowl of cold water (see Cook's Tip). Cut the potatoes into thin slices.

2 Bring a large saucepan of water to a boil and add the potato slices. Lower the heat and simmer for 5–6 minutes, or until just tender.

3 Heat the oil in a large skillet. Add the onion slices and garlic to the pan and sauté, stirring occasionally, for about 3–4 minutes.

4 Add the sun-dried tomatoes and continue cooking for a further 2 minutes.

5 Place a layer of potatoes at the bottom of a deep, ovenproof dish. Top with a layer of the onion mixture, artichokes, and ricotta cheese. Repeat the layers in the same order, finishing with a layer of potatoes on top.

6 Beat together the eggs, milk, half the Parmesan, thyme, and salt and pepper to taste and pour over the potatoes.

7 Top with the remaining Parmesan cheese and bake in a preheated oven at 375°F for 20–25 minutes, or until cooked through and golden brown. Cut into slices and serve.

COOK'S TIP

Placing the potatoes in a bowl of cold water will prevent them from turning brown while you cut the rest into slices.

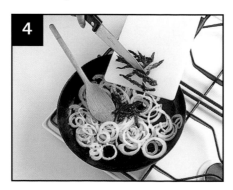

Casserole of Beans in Tomato Sauce

*This quick and easy casserole can be eaten as a healthy
supper dish or as a side dish to accompany sausages or broiled fish.*

Serves 4

INGREDIENTS

14 ounce can cannellini beans
14 ounce can borlotti beans
2 tbsp olive oil

1 celery stalk
2 garlic cloves, chopped
6 ounces baby onions, halved

1 pound tomatoes
$2^3/4$ ounces arugula

1 Drain both cans of beans and reserve 6 tbsp of the liquid.

2 Heat the oil in a large pan. Add the celery, garlic, and onions and sauté for 5 minutes, or until the onions are golden.

3 Cut a cross in the base of each tomato and plunge them into a bowl of boiling water for 30 seconds, until the skins split. Remove them with a slotted spoon and leave until cool enough to handle. Peel off the skin and chop the flesh. Add the tomato flesh and the reserved bean liquid to the pan and cook for 5 minutes.

4 Add the beans to the pan and cook for a further 3–4 minutes, or until the beans are hot.

5 Stir in the arugula and allow to wilt slightly before serving.

COOK'S TIP

Another way to peel tomatoes is to cut a cross in the base, then push it onto a fork, and hold it over a flame, turning it slowly so that the skin heats evenly all over. The skin will start to bubble and split, and should then slide off easily.

VARIATION

For a spicier tasting dish, add 1–2 teaspoons hot pepper sauce with the beans in step 4.

Small Crêpes with Smoked Fish

These are delicious as a starter or light supper dish and you can vary the filling with whichever fish you prefer.

Makes 12 crêpes

INGREDIENTS

CRÊPES:
3/4 cup all-purpose flour
1/2 tsp salt
1 egg, beaten
1 1/4 cups milk
1 tbsp oil, for frying

SAUCE:
1 pound smoked haddock, skinned
1 1/4 cups milk
3 tbsp butter or margarine
1/3 cup all-purpose flour
1 1/4 cups fish stock
1 cup grated Parmesan cheese

1 cup frozen peas, thawed
3 1/2 ounces cooked, peeled shrimp
1/2 grated Swiss cheese
salt and pepper

1 To make the crêpe batter, sift the flour and salt into a large bowl and make a well in the center. Add the egg and, using a wooden spoon, begin to draw in the flour. Slowly add the milk and beat to form a smooth batter. Set aside until required.

2 Place the fish in a skillet, add the milk, and bring to a boil. Simmer for 10 minutes, or until the fish begins to flake. Drain, reserving the milk.

3 Melt the butter in a saucepan. Add the flour, mix to a paste, and cook for 2–3 minutes. Remove the pan from the heat and add the reserved milk a little at a time, stirring to make a smooth sauce. Repeat with the fish stock. Return to the heat and bring to a boil, stirring. Stir in the Parmesan and season with salt and pepper.

4 Grease a skillet with oil. Add 2 tablespoons of the crêpe batter, swirling it around, and cook

for 2–3 minutes. Loosen the sides with a spatula and flip the crêpe over. Cook for 2–3 minutes, until golden. Repeat with the remaining batter. Stack the crêpes with sheets of baking parchment between them and keep warm in the oven.

5 Stir the fish, peas, and shrimp into half the sauce and use to fill each crêpe. Pour the remaining sauce over the crêpes, top with the Swiss cheese, and bake at 375°F for 20 minutes, until golden.

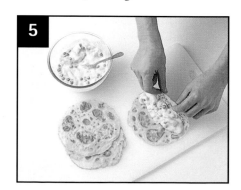

Roasted Seafood

Vegetables become deliciously sweet and juicy when they are roasted, and they go particularly well with fish and seafood.

Serves 4

INGREDIENTS

1 pound 5 ounces new potatoes
3 red onions, cut into wedges
2 zucchini, sliced into chunks

8 garlic cloves, peeled
2 lemons, cut into wedges
4 sprigs rosemary
4 tbsp olive oil

12 ounces raw shrimp
2 small squid, chopped into rings
4 tomatoes, quartered

1 Scrub the potatoes to remove any dirt. Cut any large potatoes in half. Place the potatoes in a large roasting pan, together with the onion wedges, sliced zucchini, garlic, lemon wedges, and rosemary.

2 Pour the oil over the vegetables and toss to coat all of them in the oil.

3 Cook in a preheated oven at 400°F for about 40 minutes, turning occasionally, until the potatoes are cooked through and tender.

4 Once the potatoes are tender, add the shrimp, squid, and tomatoes, tossing to coat them in the oil, and roast for 10 minutes. All the vegetables should be cooked through and slightly charred for full flavor.

5 Transfer to serving plates and serve hot.

COOK'S TIP

Squid and octopus are great favorites in Italy and all around the Mediterranean.

VARIATION

Most vegetables are suitable for roasting in the oven. Try adding 1 pound pumpkin, squash, or eggplant, if you prefer.

Omelet Strips in Tomato Sauce

These omelet strips are delicious smothered in tomato sauce.

Serves 4

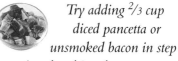

INGREDIENTS

2 tbsp butter
1 onion, finely chopped
2 garlic cloves, chopped
4 eggs, beaten

²/₃ cup milk
³/₄ cup diced Swiss cheese
14 ounce can tomatoes, chopped

1 tbsp rosemary, stalks removed
²/₃ cup vegetable stock
freshly grated Parmesan cheese, for
    sprinkling
crusty bread, to serve

1 Melt the butter in a large skillet. Add the onion and garlic and sauté for 4–5 minutes, until softened.

2 Beat together the eggs and milk and add to the skillet.

3 Using a spatula, gently raise the cooked edges of the omelet and tip any uncooked egg around the edge of the skillet.

4 Scatter the Swiss cheese over the omelet. Cook for 5 minutes, turning once, until golden on both sides. Remove from the skillet and roll up.

5 Add the chopped tomatoes, rosemary, and vegetable stock to the skillet, stirring, and bring to a boil.

6 Simmer for about 10 minutes, until reduced and thickened.

7 Slice the omelet into strips and add to the tomato sauce in the skillet. Cook for 3–4 minutes, until piping hot.

8 Sprinkle the freshly grated Parmesan cheese over the omelet strips in tomato sauce and serve with fresh crusty bread.

VARIATION

Try adding ²/₃ cup diced pancetta or unsmoked bacon in step 1 and cooking the meat with the onions.

Mozzarella Sandwiches

These deep-fried mozzarella sandwiches are a tasty snack at any time of the day, or serve smaller triangles as an antipasto with drinks.

Serves 4

INGREDIENTS

8 slices day-old bread, crusts removed
3¹/₂ ounces mozzarella cheese, thickly sliced

8 canned anchovy fillets, drained and chopped
16 fresh basil leaves
¹/₂ cup pitted black olives, chopped

4 eggs, beaten
²/₃ cup milk
oil, for deep-frying
salt and pepper

1 Cut each slice of bread into 2 triangles. Top 8 of the bread triangles with the mozzarella slices and chopped anchovies.

2 Place the basil leaves and olives on top and season with salt and pepper to taste.

3 Lay the other 8 triangles of bread over the top and press down around the edges to seal.

4 Mix the eggs and milk and pour into an ovenproof dish. Add the sandwiches and leave to soak for 5 minutes.

5 Heat the oil in a large pan until a cube of bread browns in 30 seconds—the oil will then be hot enough for deep-frying.

6 Before cooking the sandwiches, squeeze the edges together again.

7 Carefully place the sandwiches in the oil and deep-fry for 2 minutes, or until golden, turning once. Remove the sandwiches with a slotted spoon and drain on absorbent paper towels. Serve immediately while still hot.

COOK'S TIP

If desired, try adding a peeled, cooked shrimp to each triangle. For smaller sandwiches, cut the bread into 4 triangles.

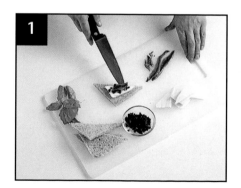

Baked Fennel

Fennel is used a lot in northern Italy. It is a very versatile vegetable, which is good cooked or in salads.

Serves 4

INGREDIENTS

2 fennel bulbs
2 celery stalks cut into 3-inch sticks

6 sun-dried tomatoes, halved
7 ounces tomato sauce

2 tsp dried oregano
$^2/_3$ cup grated Parmesan cheese

1 Using a sharp knife, trim the fennel, discarding any tough outer leaves, and cut the bulb into quarters.

2 Bring a large pan of water to a boil, add the fennel and celery, and cook for 8–10 minutes, or until just tender. Remove with a slotted spoon and drain.

3 Place the fennel pieces, celery, and sun-dried tomatoes in an ovenproof dish.

4 Mix the tomato sauce and oregano and pour the mixture over the fennel.

5 Sprinkle the Parmesan cheese on top and bake in a preheated oven at 375°F for 20 minutes or until hot.

6 Serve as a starter with fresh, crusty bread or as a vegetable side dish.

VARIATION

If you cannot find any fennel in the shops, leeks make a delicious alternative. Use about 1 pound 10 oz, chopped, making sure that they are washed thoroughly to remove all traces of soil.

VARIATION

Add a 14 ounce can lima beans, drained, in step 3 for a substantial vegetarian supper dish.

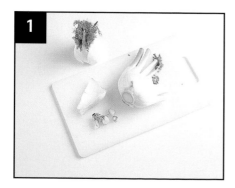

Garlic & Pine Nut Tarts

*A crisp lining of bread is filled with garlic butter
and pine nuts to make a delightful starter.*

Serves 4

INGREDIENTS

4 slices whole-wheat or granary bread	$^2/_3$ cup butter	4 black olives, halved
$^1/_2$ cup pine nuts	5 garlic cloves, peeled and halved	oregano leaves, to garnish
	2 tbsp fresh oregano	

1 Using a rolling pin, flatten the bread slightly. Using a pastry cutter, cut out 4 rounds to fit your individual tart pans—they should measure about 4 inches across. Reserve the trimmings of bread and put in the refrigerator for 10 minutes, or until required.

2 Meanwhile, spread out the pine nuts on a cookie sheet. Toast the pine nuts under a preheated broiler for 2–3 minutes, or until golden.

3 Put the bread trimmings, pine nuts, butter, garlic, and oregano into a food processor and blend for about 20 seconds. Alternatively, pound the ingredients by hand in a mortar with a pestle. The mixture should have a rough texture.

4 Spoon the pine nut butter mixture into the lined pan and top with the olives. Bake in a preheated oven at 400°F for 10–15 minutes, or until a golden brown color.

5 Transfer the tarts to serving plates and serve warm, garnished with the fresh oregano leaves.

VARIATION

Puff pastry can be used instead of the bread for the tart shells. Use 7 ounces puff pastry dough to line 4 tart pans. Chill the puff pastry dough in the refrigerator for 20 minutes. Line the tart pans with the dough and foil and bake for 10 minutes. Remove the foil and bake for a further 3–4 minutes, or until the pastry is just set. Cool, then continue from step 2, adding 2 tablespoons of bread crumbs to the mixture.

Potatoes with Olives & Anchovies

This side dish makes a delicious accompaniment for broiled fish or for lamb chops.
The fennel adds a subtle aniseed flavor.

Serves 4

INGREDIENTS

1 pound baby new potatoes, scrubbed
2 tbsp olive oil

2 fennel bulbs, trimmed and sliced
2 sprigs rosemary, stalks removed
1/2 cup mixed olives

8 canned anchovy fillets, drained

1 Bring a large saucepan of water to a boil and cook the potatoes for 8–10 minutes, or until just tender. Remove the potatoes from the saucepan using a slotted spoon and set aside to cool slightly.

2 Once the potatoes are just cool enough to handle, cut them into wedges, using a sharp knife.

3 Pit the mixed olives and cut them in half, using a sharp knife.

4 Using a sharp knife, chop the anchovy fillets into small strips.

5 Heat the oil in a large skillet. Add the potato wedges, sliced fennel, and rosemary. Cook for 7–8 minutes, or until the potatoes are golden.

6 Stir in the olives and anchovies and cook for 1 minute, or until warmed through.

7 Transfer to serving plates and serve immediately.

COOK'S TIP

Fresh rosemary is a particular favorite with Italians, but you can experiment with your own favorite herbs in this recipe.

Tuscan Chicken Livers on Toast

Crostini are small pieces of toast with a savory topping.
In Italy this is a popular antipasto dish.

Serves 4

INGREDIENTS

2 tbsp olive oil
1 garlic clove, finely chopped
8 ounces fresh or frozen chicken
   livers, thawed

2 tbsp white wine
2 tbsp lemon juice
4 fresh sage leaves, finely chopped or
   1 tsp dried, crumbled sage

salt and pepper
4 slices ciabatta or other Italian
   bread
wedges of lemon, to garnish

1 Heat the olive oil in a skillet and sauté the garlic for 1 minute.

2 Rinse and roughly chop the chicken livers, using a sharp knife.

3 Add the chicken livers to the skillet, together with the white wine and lemon juice. Cook for 3–4 minutes, or until the juices from the chicken livers run clear.

4 Stir in the sage and season to taste with salt and pepper.

5 Toast the bread under a preheated broiler for 2 minutes on both sides, or until golden brown.

6 Spoon the hot chicken livers on top of the toasted bread and serve garnished with a wedge of lemon.

COOK'S TIP

Overcooked liver is dry and tasteless. Cook the chopped liver for only 3–4 minutes—it should be soft and tender.

VARIATION

Another way to make crostini is to slice a crusty loaf or a French loaf into small rounds or squares. Heat the olive oil in a skillet and fry the slices of bread until golden brown and crisp on both sides. Remove the crostini from the pan with a slotted spoon and drain thoroughly on paper towels. Top with the chicken livers.

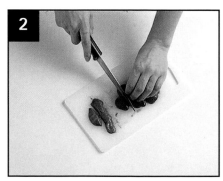

Onion & Mozarella Tarts

These individual tarts are delicious hot or cold and are great for picnics.

Serves 4

INGREDIENTS

9 ounces ready-made puff pastry
dough, defrosted if frozen
2 medium red onions

1 red bell pepper
8 cherry tomatoes, halved

3 ³/₄ ounces mozzarella cheese, cut
into chunks
8 sprigs thyme

1 Roll out the dough to make
4 x 3-inch squares. Using a
sharp knife, trim the edges of the
dough, reserving the trimmings.
Chill the dough in the refrigerator
for 30 minutes.

2 Place the dough squares on a
cookie sheet. Brush a little
water along each edge of the
dough squares and use the
reserved dough trimmings to
make a rim around each tart.

3 Using a sharp knife, cut the
red onions into wedges
and halve and seed the red
bell pepper.

4 Place the onions and bell
pepper in a roasting pan.
Cook under a preheated broiler for
15 minutes or until charred.

5 Place the roasted bell pepper
halves in a plastic bag and set
aside to sweat for 10 minutes.
Carefully peel off the skin from
the bell pepper and cut the flesh
into strips.

6 Line the dough squares with
squares of foil. Bake in a
preheated oven at 400°F for
10 minutes. Remove the foil
squares and bake for a further
5 minutes.

7 Place the onions, bell pepper
strips, tomatoes, and cheese in
each tart and sprinkle with the
fresh thyme.

8 Bake in the oven for
15 minutes, or until the pastry
is golden. Serve hot.

Pasta & Rice

Easy to cook and easy on the wallet, pasta is wonderfully versatile. It can be served with meat, fish, or vegetable sauces, or baked in the oven. Some of the most popular and best-known pasta dishes are those that combine long strands of pasta cooked "al dente," with a rich, hearty meat sauce, such as Spaghetti Bolognese, which needs no introduction. Fish and seafood are irresistible combined with pasta and need only the briefest of cooking times. Pasta combined with vegetables provides inspiration for countless dishes that will please vegetarians and meat-eaters alike.

Rice dishes are very popular in the north of Italy—they are particularly fond of risottos. Milanese and other risottos are made with short-grain rice, the best of which is arborio—this type of rice should be rinsed before using. An Italian risotto is far moister than pilau or other savory rice dishes, but it should not be soggy.

Gnocchi are made with maize flour, cornmeal (polenta), potatoes, or cream of wheat, often combined with spinach or some sort of cheese. Gnocchi resemble dumplings and are either poached or baked, and served with a sauce. Polenta is made with either cornmeal or polenta flour and can be served as a soft porridge or a firmer cake, which is then fried until crisp.

Tagliatelle with Garlic Butter

Pasta is not difficult to make yourself, just a little time-consuming. The resulting pasta takes only a couple of minutes to cook and it tastes wonderful.

Serves 4

INGREDIENTS

1 pound strong white flour, plus extra for dredging	4 eggs, beaten	3 garlic cloves, finely chopped
2 tsp salt	3 tbsp olive oil	2 tbsp chopped, fresh parsley
	5 tbsp butter, melted	pepper

1 Sift the flour into a large bowl and stir in the salt.

2 Make a well in the middle of the dry ingredients and add the eggs and 2 tablespoons of oil. Using a wooden spoon, stir in the eggs, gradually drawing in the flour. After a few minutes the dough will be too stiff to use a spoon and you will need to use your fingers.

3 Once all of the flour has been incorporated, turn the dough out onto a floured surface and knead for about 5 minutes, until smooth and elastic. If you find the dough is too wet, add a little more flour and continue kneading. Cover the dough with plastic wrap and set aside to rest for at least 15 minutes.

4 The basic dough is now ready. Roll the dough out thinly and create the pasta shapes required. This can be done by hand or with the aid of a pasta machine. The results from a machine are usually neater and thinner, but not necessarily better.

5 To make the tagliatelle by hand, fold the thinly rolled pasta sheets into 3 and, with a sharp knife, cut out long, thin strips, about ½ inch wide.

6 To cook, bring a large pan of water to a boil, add 1 tablespoon of oil and the pasta. It will take 2–3 minutes to cook, and the texture should have a slight bite to it. Drain thoroughly.

7 Mix together the butter, garlic, and parsley. Stir into the pasta and serve immediately with plenty of black pepper.

COOK'S TIP

Generally allow about 5½ ounces fresh pasta or about 3½ ounces dried pasta per person.

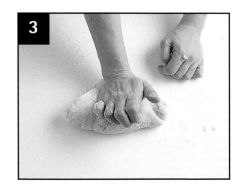

Spaghetti Bolognese

This classic dish is still a favorite in Bologna. The original recipe takes about four hours to cook and should be left overnight to allow the flavors to mingle. This version is much quicker.

Serves 4

INGREDIENTS

1 tbsp olive oil
1 onion, finely chopped
2 garlic cloves, chopped
1 carrot, peeled and chopped
1 celery stalk, chopped

$^1/_3$ cup diced pancetta or bacon
12 ounces lean ground beef
14 ounce can chopped tomatoes

2 tsp dried oregano
$^1/_2$ cup red wine
2 tbsp tomato paste
salt and pepper
$1^1/_2$ pounds fresh spaghetti or
    12 ounces dried spaghetti

1 Heat the oil in a large skillet. Add the onions and sauté for 3 minutes.

2 Add the garlic, carrot, celery, and pancetta or bacon and sauté for 3–4 minutes, or until just beginning to brown.

3 Add the beef and cook over a high heat for another 3 minutes, or until all of the meat is brown.

4 Stir in the tomatoes, oregano, and red wine and bring to a boil. Reduce the heat and simmer for about 45 minutes.

5 Stir in the tomato paste and season with salt and pepper.

6 Cook the spaghetti in a pan of boiling water according to the instructions on the packet, or until it is cooked, but still has "bite." Drain thoroughly.

7 Transfer the spaghetti to a serving dish and pour the Bolognese sauce over it. Toss to mix well and serve hot.

VARIATION

Try adding 1ounce dried porcini, soaked for 10 minutes in 2 tablespoons warm water, to the Bolognese sauce in step 4, if you wish.

COOK'S TIP

The sauce can be stored in the freezer for 2 months or in the refrigerator for 2–3 days.

Spicy Tomato Tagliatelle

*A deliciously fresh and slightly spicy tomato sauce which
is excellent for lunch or a light supper.*

Serves 4

INGREDIENTS

3 tbsp butter
1 onion, finely chopped
1 garlic clove, crushed
2 small fresh red chilies, seeded
and diced

1 pound fresh tomatoes, skinned,
seeded, and diced
³/4 cup vegetable stock
2 tbsp tomato paste
1 tsp sugar

salt and pepper
1¹/2 pounds fresh green and white
tagliatelle, or 12 ounces dried

1 Melt the butter in a large
saucepan. Add the onion and
garlic and sauté for 3–4 minutes,
or until softened.

2 Add the chilies to the pan and
continue cooking for about
2 minutes.

3 Add the tomatoes and stock,
reduce the heat, and simmer
for 10 minutes, stirring.

4 Pour the sauce into a food
processor and blend for
1 minute, until smooth.

Alternatively, push the sauce
through a strainer.

5 Return the sauce to the pan
and add the tomato paste,
sugar, and salt and pepper to taste.
Gently reheat over a low heat,
until piping hot.

6 Cook the tagliatelle in a pan
of boiling water according to
the instructions on the packet or
until it is cooked, but still has
"bite." Drain the tagliatelle,
transfer to serving plates, and serve
with the tomato sauce.

VARIATION

*Try topping your pasta
dish with ¹/3 cup diced
pancetta or unsmoked
bacon, dry-fried for
5 minutes, until crispy.*

Basil & Tomato Pasta

Roasting the tomatoes gives a sweeter and smoother flavor to this sauce. Try to buy
Italian tomatoes, such as plum or flavia, as these have a better flavor and color.

Serves 4

INGREDIENTS

1 tbsp olive oil
2 sprigs rosemary
2 cloves garlic, unpeeled

1 pound tomatoes, halved
1 tbsp sun-dried tomato paste
12 fresh basil leaves, plus extra to
garnish

salt and pepper
1^{1}/2 pounds fresh farfalle or
12 ounces dried farfalle

1 Place the rosemary, garlic, and tomatoes, skin side up, in a roasting pan, with half of the oil.

2 Drizzle with the remaining oil and cook under a preheated broiler for 20 minutes, or until the tomato skins are slightly charred.

3 Peel the skin from the tomatoes. Roughly chop the tomato flesh and place in a pan.

4 Squeeze the pulp from the garlic cloves and mix with the tomato flesh and sun-dried tomato paste.

5 Roughly tear the fresh basil leaves into smaller pieces and then stir them into the sauce. Season with a little salt and pepper to taste.

6 Cook the farfalle in a saucepan of boiling water according to the instructions on the packet, or until it is cooked through, but still has "bite." Drain.

7 Gently heat the tomato and basil sauce.

8 Transfer the farfalle to serving plates and serve with the basil and tomato sauce.

COOK'S TIP

This sauce tastes just as good
when served cold in a
pasta salad.

Pasta Vongole

Fresh clams are available from most good fish stores. If you prefer, used canned clams, which are less messy to eat but not so pretty to serve.

Serves 4

INGREDIENTS

$1^1/_2$ pounds fresh clams or 10 ounce
   can clams, drained
14 ounces mixed seafood, such as
   shrimps, squid, and mussels,
   thawed if frozen

2 tbsp olive oil
2 cloves garlic, finely chopped
$^2/_3$ cup white wine
$^2/_3$ cup fish stock
2 tbsp chopped tarragon

salt and pepper
$1^1/_2$ pounds fresh pasta or
   12 ounces dried pasta

1   If you are using fresh clams, scrub them clean and discard any that are already open.

2   Heat the oil in a large skillet. Add the garlic and the clams to the pan and cook for 2 minutes, shaking the pan to ensure that all the clams are coated in the oil.

3   Add the remaining seafood mixture to the skillet and cook for a further 2 minutes.

4   Pour the wine and stock over the mixed seafood, and bring to a boil. Cover the skillet, reduce the heat, and simmer for 8–10 minutes, or until the shells open. Discard any clams or mussels that do not open.

5   Meanwhile, cook the pasta in a saucepan of boiling water according to the instructions on the packet, or until it is cooked through, but still has "bite." Drain.

6   Stir the tarragon into the sauce and season to taste.

7   Transfer the pasta to a serving dish, pour the sauce over it, and serve.

VARIATION

Red clam sauce can be made by adding 8 tablespoons of tomato sauce along with the stock in step 4. Follow the same cooking method.

Basil & Pine Nut Pesto

Delicious stirred into pasta, soups, and salad dressings, pesto is available from most supermarkets, but making your own gives a much fresher, fuller flavor.

Serves 4

INGREDIENTS

about 40 fresh basil leaves
3 garlic cloves, crushed
$^1/_4$ cup pine nuts

$^2/_3$ cup finely grated Parmesan
cheese
2–3 tbsp extra-virgin olive oil
salt and pepper

1$^1/_2$ pounds fresh pasta or
12 ounces dried pasta

1 Rinse the basil leaves and pat them dry with paper towels.

2 Put the basil leaves, garlic, pine nuts, and grated Parmesan into a food processor and blend for about 30 seconds, or until smooth. Alternatively, pound the ingredients by hand, using a mortar and pestle.

3 If you are using a food processor, keep the motor running and slowly add the olive oil. Alternatively, add the oil drop by drop while stirring briskly. Season with salt and pepper.

4 Meanwhile, cook the pasta in a saucepan of boiling water according to the instructions on the packet, or until it is cooked through, but still has "bite." Drain.

5 Transfer the pasta to a serving dish and add the pesto. Toss to mix well and serve hot.

VARIATION

Try making a walnut version of this pesto. Substitute $^1/_4$ cup walnuts for the pine nuts and add 1 tablespoon walnut oil in step 2.

COOK'S TIP

You can store pesto in the refrigerator for about 4 weeks. Cover the surface of the pesto with olive oil before sealing the container or bottle, to prevent the basil from oxidizing and turning black.

Chili & Bell Pepper Pasta

This roasted bell pepper and chili sauce is sweet and spicy.

Serves 4

INGREDIENTS

2 red bell peppers, halved and seeded
1 small fresh red chili
2 garlic cloves
4 tomatoes, halved

$1/2$ cup ground almonds
7 tbsp olive oil

$1^1/2$ pounds fresh pasta or
   12 ounces dried pasta
fresh oregano leaves, to garnish

1 Place the bell peppers, skin side up, on a cookie sheet with the chili, garlic, and tomatoes. Cook under a preheated broiler for 15 minutes, or until charred. After 10 minutes turn the tomatoes skin side up.

2 Place the bell peppers and chilies in a plastic bag and set aside to sweat for 10 minutes.

3 Remove the skin from the bell peppers and chilies and slice the flesh into strips, using a sharp knife.

4 Peel the garlic and peel and seed the tomatoes.

5 Spread out the almonds on a cookie sheet and place under the broiler for 2–3 minutes, until golden.

6 Using a food processor, blend the bell pepper, chili, garlic, and tomatoes to make a purée. Keep the motor running and slowly add the olive oil to form a thick sauce. Alternatively, mash the mixture with a fork and beat in the olive oil, drop by drop.

7 Stir the toasted ground almonds into the mixture.

8 Warm the sauce in a saucepan until it is heated through.

9 Cook the pasta in a saucepan of boiling water according to the instructions on the packet, or until it is cooked through, but still has "bite." Drain the pasta and transfer to a serving dish. Pour the sauce on top and toss to mix. Garnish with fresh oregano leaves.

VARIATION

Add 2 tablespoons red wine vinegar to the sauce and use as a dressing for a cold pasta salad, if you wish.

Pasta Carbonara

Lightly cooked eggs and pancetta are combined with cheese to make this rich, classic sauce.

Serves 4

INGREDIENTS

1 tbsp olive oil
3 tbsp butter
²/₃ cup diced pancetta or unsmoked
   bacon

3 eggs, beaten
2 tbsp milk
1 tbsp thyme, stalks removed
1¹/₂ pounds fresh or 12 ounces dried
   conchigoni rigati

salt and pepper
²/₃ cup grated Parmesan cheese

---

1 Heat the oil and butter in a skillet until the mixture is just beginning to froth.

2 Add the pancetta or bacon to the pan and cook for 5 minutes, or until well browned.

3 Mix together the eggs and milk in a small bowl. Stir in the thyme and season to taste with salt and pepper.

4 Cook the pasta in a saucepan of boiling water according to the instructions on the packet or until it is cooked through, but still has "bite." Drain thoroughly.

5 Add the cooked, drained pasta to the skillet with the eggs and cook over a high heat for about 30 seconds until the eggs just begin to cook and set. Do not overcook the eggs or they will become rubbery.

6 Stir in half the grated Parmesan cheese.

7 Transfer the pasta to a serving dish, pour the sauce on top, and toss to mix well.

8 Sprinkle the rest of the grated Parmesan over the top and serve immediately.

VARIATION

For an extra rich carbonara sauce, stir in 4 tablespoons heavy cream with the eggs and milk in step 2. Follow exactly the same cooking method.

Pasta & Sicilian Sauce

*This Sicilian recipe of anchovies mixed with pine nuts
and golden raisins in a tomato sauce is delicious with all types of pasta.*

Serves 4

INGREDIENTS

1 pound tomatoes, halved
1/4 cup pine nuts
1/3 cup golden raisins

1 3/4 ounce can anchovies, drained
and halved lengthwise
2 tbsp concentrated tomato paste

1 1/2 pounds fresh or
12 ounces dried penne

1 Cook the tomatoes under a preheated broiler for about 10 minutes. Cool slightly, then once cool enough to handle, carefully peel off the skin and dice the flesh, using a sharp knife.

2 Place the pine nuts on a cookie sheet and lightly toast under the broiler for 2–3 minutes or until golden.

3 Soak the golden raisins in a bowl of warm water for about 20 minutes. Drain the raisins thoroughly.

4 Place the tomatoes, pine nuts, and golden raisins in a small pan and gently heat.

5 Add the anchovies and tomato paste, heating the sauce for a further 2–3 minutes, or until hot.

6 Cook the pasta in a saucepan of boiling water according to the instructions on the packet, or until it is cooked through, but still has "bite." Drain thoroughly.

7 Transfer the pasta to a serving plate and serve with the hot Sicilian sauce.

VARIATION

Add 3 1/2 ounces bacon, broiled for 5 minutes, until crispy, then chopped, instead of the anchovies, if you prefer.

COOK'S TIP

If you are making fresh pasta (see page 100), remember that pasta dough prefers warm conditions and responds well to handling. Do not chill and do not use a marble surface for kneading.

Chicken Lasagne

This variation of the traditional beef dish has layers of pasta and chicken or turkey baked in red wine, tomatoes, and a delicious cheese sauce.

Serves 4

INGREDIENTS

12 ounces fresh lasagne (about 9 sheets) or 5^1/$_2$ ounces dried lasagne (about 9 sheets)
1 tbsp olive oil
1 red onion, finely chopped
1 garlic clove, crushed
1^1/$_2$ cups sliced mushrooms

12 ounces skinless chicken or turkey breast, cut into chunks
2$/_3$ cup red wine, diluted with ^{1}/$_3$ cup water
9 ounces tomato sauce
1 tsp sugar

BÉCHAMEL SAUCE:
5 tbsp butter
^{1}/$_2$ cup all-purpose flour
2^1/$_2$ cups milk
1 egg, beaten
1 cup grated Parmesan cheese
salt and pepper

1 Cook the lasagne in a pan of boiling water according to the instructions on the packet. Lightly grease a deep ovenproof dish.

2 Heat the oil in a pan. Add the onion and garlic and sauté for 3–4 minutes. Add the mushrooms and chicken and stir-fry for 4 minutes, or until the meat browns.

3 Add the wine, bring to a boil, then lower the heat and simmer for 5 minutes. Stir in the tomato sauce and sugar and cook for 3–5 minutes, until the meat is tender and cooked through. The sauce should have thickened, but still be quite runny.

4 To make the béchamel sauce, melt the butter in a pan, stir in the flour, and cook for 2 minutes. Remove the pan from the heat and gradually add the milk, mixing to form a smooth sauce. Return the pan to the heat and bring to a boil, stirring until thickened. Cool slightly, then beat in the egg and half the cheese. Season to taste.

5 Place 3 sheets of lasagne in the base of the dish and cover with half the chicken mixture. Repeat the layers. Finish with the last 3 sheets of lasagne, pour the béchamel sauce on top, and sprinkle with the Parmesan. Bake in a preheated oven at 375°F for 30 minutes, until golden.

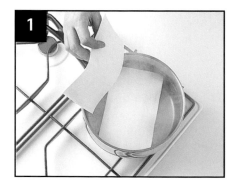

Cannelloni

It is easier to use dried pasta in this recipe—you can buy it ready-made in tubes.
If you are using fresh pasta (see page 100), you must cut out squares and roll them yourself.

Serves 4

INGREDIENTS

20 tubes dried cannelloni (about
   7 oz) or 20 square sheets of fresh
   pasta (about 12 oz)
1$^{1}/_{8}$ cups ricotta cheese
5$^{1}/_{2}$ ounces frozen spinach, thawed

$^{1}/_{2}$ small red bell pepper, seeded
   and diced
2 scallions, chopped
$^{2}/_{3}$ cup hot vegetable or
   chicken stock

1 portion of basil and tomato sauce
   (see page 106)
$^{1}/_{3}$ cup grated Parmesan or pecorino
   cheese
salt and pepper

1 If you are using dried cannelloni, check the packet instructions; many varieties do not need pre-cooking. If necessary, pre-cook your pasta. Bring a large saucepan of water to a boil, add 1 tablespoon oil, and cook the pasta for 3–4 minutes—it is easier to do this in batches. Drain thoroughly.

2 In a bowl, mix together the ricotta, spinach, bell pepper, and scallions and season to taste with salt and pepper.

3 Lightly butter an ovenproof dish, large enough to contain all the pasta tubes in a single layer. Spoon the ricotta and spinach mixture into the pasta tubes and place them into the prepared dish. If you are using fresh sheets of pasta, spread the ricotta mixture along one side of each fresh pasta square and roll up to form a tube.

4 Mix together the stock and basil and tomato sauce (see page 106) and pour over the pasta tubes.

5 Sprinkle the cheese over the cannelloni and bake in a preheated oven at 375°F for 20–25 minutes, or until the pasta is cooked through.

VARIATION

If you would prefer a creamier version, omit the stock and the basil and tomato sauce and replace with béchamel sauce (see page 118).

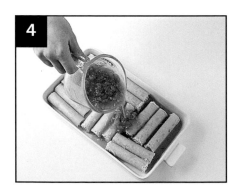

Tortellini

These tasty little squares of pasta stuffed with mushrooms and cheese are surprisingly filling. Serve about three pieces for a starter and up to nine for a main course.

Makes 36 pieces

INGREDIENTS

about 10^1/$_2$ ounces fresh pasta (see page 100), rolled out to thin sheets
5 tbsp butter
4 tbsp finely chopped shallots

3 garlic cloves, crushed
^{3}/$_4$ cup finely chopped mushrooms
^{1}/$_2$ celery stalk, finely chopped

^{1}/$_3$ cup finely grated pecorino cheese, plus extra to garnish
1 tbsp oil
salt and pepper

1 Using a serrated pasta cutter, cut 2-inch squares from the sheets of fresh pasta. To make 36 tortellini you will need 72 squares. Once the pasta is cut, cover the squares with plastic wrap to keep them from drying out.

2 Heat 3 tbsp of the butter in a skillet. Add the shallots, 1 crushed garlic clove, the mushrooms, and celery, and cook for 4–5 minutes.

3 Remove the pan from the heat, stir in the cheese, and season with salt and pepper.

4 Spoon ^{1}/$_2$ teaspoon of the mixture onto the middle of 36 pasta squares. Brush the edges of the squares with water and top with the remaining 36 squares. Press the edges together to seal. Set aside to rest for 5 minutes.

5 Bring a large pan of water to a boil, add the oil, and cook the tortellini, in batches, for 2–3 minutes. The tortellini will rise to the surface when cooked and the pasta should be tender with a slight "bite." Remove from the pan with a slotted spoon and drain thoroughly.

6 Meanwhile, melt the remaining butter in a pan. Add the remaining garlic and plenty of pepper and cook for 1–2 minutes.

7 Transfer the tortellini to serving plates and pour the garlic butter over them. Garnish with grated pecorino cheese and serve immediately.

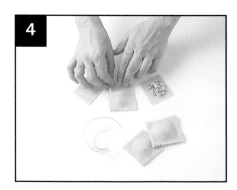

Chili Polenta Fries

Polenta is a maize flour used in Italy in the same way as potatoes and rice. On its own it has little flavor, but combined with butter, garlic, and herbs, it is completely transformed.

Serves 4

INGREDIENTS

3 cups instant polenta
2 tsp chili powder

1 tbsp olive oil
$^2/_3$ cup sour cream

1 tbsp chopped parsley
salt and pepper

1 Bring 6¼ cups water to a boil in a large saucepan. Add 2 teaspoons salt and then add the polenta in a steady stream, stirring constantly.

2 Reduce the heat slightly and continue stirring for about 5 minutes. It is essential to stir the polenta, otherwise it will stick to the bottom of the pan and burn. The polenta should have a thick consistency at this point and should be stiff enough to hold the spoon upright in the pan.

3 Add the chili powder to the polenta mixture and stir well. Season to taste with a little salt and pepper.

4 Spread the polenta out on to a board or cookie sheet to about 1½ inches thick. Let cool and set.

5 Cut the cooled polenta mixture into thin wedges.

6 Heat 1 tablespoon of oil in a pan. Add the polenta wedges and fry for 3–4 minutes on each side until golden and crispy. Alternatively, brush with melted butter and broil for 6–7 minutes, until golden. Drain the cooked polenta on paper towels.

7 Mix the sour cream with parsley and place in a small serving bowl.

8 Serve the polenta with the sour cream and parsley dip.

COOK'S TIP

Easy-cook instant polenta is widely available in supermarkets and is quick to make. It will keep for up to 1 week in the refrigerator. The polenta can also be baked in a preheated oven at 400°F for 20 minutes.

Polenta Kabobs

Here, skewers of thyme-flavored polenta, wrapped
in prosciutto, are broiled or barbecued.

Serves 4

INGREDIENTS

3 cups water
1 1/2 cups instant polenta
2 tbsp fresh thyme, stalks removed

8 slices prosciutto (about
    2 3/4 ounces)
1 tbsp olive oil

salt and pepper
salad greens, to serve

1 Bring the water to a boil and add 1 teaspoon salt. Add the polenta in a steady stream, stirring constantly. Cook, stirring, for 5 minutes, or according to the instructions on the packet.

2 Add the fresh thyme to the polenta mixture and season to taste with salt and pepper.

3 Spread out the polenta, about 1 inch thick, on a board. Set aside to cool.

4 Using a sharp knife, cut the cooled polenta into 1-inch cubes.

5 Cut the prosciutto slices into 2 pieces lengthwise. Wrap the prosciutto around the polenta cubes.

6 Thread the prosciutto-wrapped polenta cubes onto skewers.

7 Brush the kabobs with a little oil and cook under a preheated broiler, turning frequently, for 7–8 minutes. Alternatively, barbecue the kabobs until golden. Transfer to serving plates and serve with salad greens.

VARIATION

Try flavoring the polenta with chopped oregano, basil, or marjoram instead of the thyme, if you prefer. You should use 3 tablespoons chopped herbs to every 3 cups instant polenta.

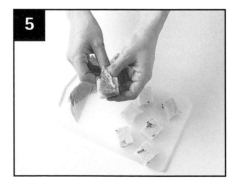

Smoked Cod Polenta

Using polenta as a crust for a gratin dish gives a lovely crispy outer texture and a smooth inside. It works well with smoked fish and chicken.

Serves 4

INGREDIENTS

6¹/₄ cups water

3 cups instant polenta

7 ounces chopped frozen spinach, thawed

3 tbsp butter

²/₃ cup grated pecorino cheese

³/₄ cup milk

1 pound skinless smoked cod fillet

4 eggs, beaten

salt and pepper

1 Bring the water to a boil and add 2 teaspoons salt. Add the polenta in a steady stream, stirring constantly. Cook, stirring, for 5 minutes, or according to the instructions on the packet.

2 Stir the spinach, butter, and half the pecorino cheese into the polenta. Season to taste with salt and pepper.

3 Divide the polenta between 4 individual ovenproof dishes, spreading the polenta evenly across the bases and up the sides of the dishes.

4 In a large skillet, bring the milk to a boil. Add the smoked cod and cook, turning once, for 8–10 minutes, or until tender. Remove the fish with a slotted spoon.

5 Remove the pan from the heat. Mix the milk and eggs together.

6 Using a fork, flake the fish into small pieces and place it in the center of the dishes.

7 Pour the milk and egg mixture over the fish.

8 Sprinkle the remaining cheese on top and bake in a preheated oven at 375°F for 25–30 minutes, or until set and golden. Serve hot.

VARIATION

Try using 12 ounces cooked chicken breast with 2 tablespoons chopped tarragon, instead of the fish.

Milanese Sun-dried Tomato Risotto

A Milanese risotto can be cooked in a variety of ways—but always with saffron.
This version with sun-dried tomatoes and wine has a lovely tangy flavor.

Serves 4

INGREDIENTS

1 tbsp olive oil	about 15 strands saffron	8 sun-dried tomatoes, cut into strips
2 tbsp butter	$^2/_3$ cup white wine	1 cup frozen peas, thawed
1 large onion, finely chopped	$3^3/_4$ cups hot vegetable or chicken	$^1/_3$ cup shredded prosciutto
$1^2/_3$ cups risotto rice, washed	stock	1 cup grated Parmesan cheese

1 Heat the oil and butter in a large skillet. Add the onion and sauté for 4–5 minutes, or until softened.

2 Add the rice and saffron to the skillet, stirring well to coat the rice in the oil, and cook for 1 minute.

3 Add the wine and stock slowly to the rice mixture in the pan, a ladleful at a time, stirring and making sure that all the liquid is absorbed before adding the next ladleful of liquid.

4 About halfway through adding the stock, stir in the tomatoes.

5 When all the wine and stock is incorporated, the rice should be cooked. Test by tasting a grain—if it is still crunchy, add a little more water and continue cooking. It should take at least 15 minutes to cook.

6 Stir in the peas, prosciutto, and cheese. Cook for 2–3 minutes, stirring, until hot. Serve with extra Parmesan.

COOK'S TIP

Italian rice is a round, short-grained variety with a nutty flavor, which is essential for a good risotto. Arborio is the very best kind to use. The finished dish should have moist, but separate grains. This is achieved by adding the hot stock a little at a time, adding more only when the last addition is fully absorbed. Don't leave the risotto to cook by itself: it needs constant watching to see when more liquid is required.

Mushroom Risotto

This creamy risotto is flavored with a mixture of exotic and cultivated mushrooms and thyme.

Serves 4

INGREDIENTS

2 tbsp olive oil
1 large onion, finely chopped
1 garlic clove, crushed
7 ounces mixed mushrooms, such as
   ceps, oyster, porcini, and button,
   wiped and sliced if large

$1^1/_3$ cups risotto rice, washed
pinch saffron threads
3 cups hot vegetable stock
$^2/_3$ cup white wine
1 cup grated Parmesan cheese, plus
   extra for serving

2 tbsp chopped thyme
salt and pepper

1 Heat the oil in a large skillet. Add the onions and garlic and sauté for 3–4 minutes, or until softened.

2 Add the mushrooms to the skillet and cook for a further 3 minutes, or until they are just beginning to brown.

3 Add the rice and saffron to the skillet and stir to coat the rice in the oil.

4 Mix together the stock and wine and add to the skillet, a ladleful at a time. Stir the rice mixture and allow the liquid to be fully absorbed before adding more liquid, a ladleful at a time.

5 When all the wine and stock is incorporated, the rice should be cooked. Test by tasting a grain—if it is still crunchy, add a little more water and continue cooking. It should take at least 15 minutes to cook.

6 Stir in the cheese and thyme, and season with freshly ground black pepper.

7 Transfer the risotto to serving dishes and serve sprinkled with extra Parmesan cheese.

COOK'S TIP

Exotic mushrooms each have their own distinctive flavors and make a change from button mushrooms. However, they can be quite expensive, so you can always use a mixture with crimini or button mushrooms instead.

Genoese Seafood Risotto

The Genoese risotto is cooked in a different way from any of the other risottos. First, you cook the rice, then you prepare a sauce, then you mix the two together. The results are just as delicious though!

Serves 4

INGREDIENTS

5 cups hot fish or chicken stock
1²/₃ cups risotto rice, washed
3 tbsp butter

2 garlic cloves, chopped
9 ounces mixed, preferably raw, seafood, such as jumbo shrimp, squid, mussels, clams, and small shrimp

2 tbsp chopped oregano, plus extra for garnishing
²/₃ cup grated pecorino or Parmesan cheese

1 In a large saucepan, bring the stock to a boil. Add the rice and cook, stirring, for about 12 minutes, until the rice is tender or according to the instructions on the packet. Drain thoroughly, reserving any excess liquid.

2 Heat the butter in a large skillet and add the garlic, stirring.

3 Add the raw mixed seafood to the skillet and cook for 5 minutes. If the seafood is already cooked, sauté for 2–3 minutes.

4 Stir the oregano into the seafood mixture in the skillet.

5 Add the cooked rice to the skillet and cook, stirring constantly, for 2–3 minutes, or until heated through. Add the reserved stock if the mixture gets too sticky.

6 Add the pecorino or Parmesan cheese and mix well.

7 Transfer the risotto to warm serving dishes and serve immediately.

COOK'S TIP

The Genoese are excellent cooks, and they make particularly delicious fish dishes flavored with the local olive oil.

Risotto-stuffed Bell Peppers

Sweet roasted bell peppers are delightful containers for a creamy risotto and especially good topped with mozzarella cheese.

Serves 4

INGREDIENTS

4 red or orange bell peppers
1 tbsp olive oil
1 large onion, finely chopped
1²/₃ cups risotto rice, washed
about 15 strands saffron
²/₃ cup white wine

3³/₄ cups hot vegetable
  or chicken stock
3 tbsp butter
²/₃ cup grated pecorino cheese,

1³/₄ ounces Italian sausage, such as
  Felino salami or other coarse
  Italian salami, chopped
7 ounces mozzarella cheese, sliced

1 Cut the bell peppers in half, leaving some of the stalk. Remove the seeds.

2 Place the bell peppers, cut side up, under a preheated broiler for 12–15 minutes, until softened and charred.

3 Meanwhile, heat the oil in a large skillet. Add the onion and sauté for 3–4 minutes, or until softened. Add the rice and saffron, stirring to coat in the oil, and cook for 1 minute.

4 Add the wine and stock slowly, a ladleful at a time, making sure that all the liquid is absorbed before adding the next ladleful of liquid. When all the liquid is absorbed, the rice should be cooked. Test by tasting a grain—if it is still crunchy, add a little more water and continue cooking. It should take at least 15 minutes to cook.

5 Stir in the butter, pecorino cheese, and the chopped Italian sausage.

6 Spoon the risotto into the bell peppers. Top with a slice of mozzarella and broil for 4–5 minutes, or until the cheese is bubbling. Serve hot.

VARIATION

Use tomatoes instead of the bell peppers, if you prefer. Halve 4 large tomatoes and scoop out the seeds. Follow steps 3–6, as there is no need to roast them.

Potato Gnocchi with Tomato Sauce

*Freshly made potato gnocchi are delicious, especially when they are
topped with a fragrant tomato sauce.*

Serves 4

INGREDIENTS

12 ounces mealy potatoes, halved
²/₃ cup self-rising flour, plus extra for
 rolling out
2 tsp dried oregano
2 tbsp oil
1 large onion, chopped

2 garlic cloves, chopped
14 ounce can chopped tomatoes
¹/₂ vegetable stock cube dissolved in
 ¹/₃ cup boiling water
salt and pepper

2 tbsp basil, shredded, plus whole
 leaves to garnish
Parmesan cheese, grated, to serve

1 Bring a large pan of water to a boil. Add the potatoes and cook for 12–15 minutes, or until tender. Drain and cool.

2 Peel and then mash the potatoes with the salt and pepper, sifted flour, and oregano. Mix together with your hands to form a dough.

3 Heat the oil in a pan. Add the onions and garlic and sauté for 3–4 minutes. Add the tomatoes and stock and cook,

uncovered, for 10 minutes. Season with salt and pepper to taste.

4 Roll the potato dough into a sausage about 1 inch in diameter. Cut the sausage into 1-inch lengths. Flour your hands, then press a fork into each piece to create a series of ridges on one side and the indent of your index finger on the other.

5 Bring a large pan of water to a boil and cook the gnocchi, in batches, for 2–3 minutes. They

should rise to the surface when cooked. Drain and keep warm.

6 Stir the basil into the tomato sauce and pour over the gnocchi. Garnish with basil leaves and freshly ground black pepper. Sprinkle with Parmesan and serve.

VARIATION

Try serving the gnocchi with Pesto Sauce (see page 110) for a change.

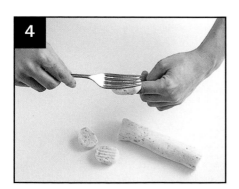

Baked Gnocchi

Cream of wheat has a similar texture to polenta, but is slightly grainier. These gnocchi, which are delicately flavored with cheese and thyme, are easy to make.

Serves 4

INGREDIENTS

1³/₄ cups vegetable stock
²/₃ cup cream of wheat
1 tbsp thyme, stalks removed
1 egg, beaten

²/₃ cup grated Parmesan cheese
3 tbsp butter
2 garlic cloves, crushed
salt and pepper

1 Place the stock in a large saucepan and bring to a boil. Add the cream of wheat in a steady trickle, stirring continuously. Keep stirring for 3–4 minutes, until the mixture is thick enough to hold a spoon upright. Set the mixture aside to cool slightly.

2 Add the thyme, egg, and half the cheese, and season to taste with salt and pepper.

3 Spread the mixture on a board in a layer about ¹/₂ inch thick. Set aside to cool and set.

4 When the mixture is cold, cut it into 1-inch squares, reserving any trimmings.

5 Grease an ovenproof dish, placing the reserved trimmings in the bottom. Arrange the cream of wheat squares on top and sprinkle with the remaining cheese.

6 Melt the butter in a pan and add the garlic and black pepper to taste. Pour the butter mixture over the gnocchi. Bake in a preheated oven at 425°F for 15–20 minutes, until puffed up and golden. Serve hot.

VARIATION

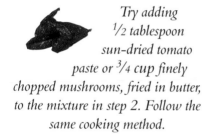

Try adding ¹/₂ tablespoon sun-dried tomato paste or ³/₄ cup finely chopped mushrooms, fried in butter, to the mixture in step 2. Follow the same cooking method.

Main Dishes

*These recipes feature exciting and tempting
ways of cooking fish and meat to make a range of
satisfying meals that are typically Italian. After pasta,
fish is probably the most important source of food in
Italy. Fish markets in Italy are fascinating, with a huge
variety of fish on display, but as most fish comes from
the Mediterranean it is not always easy to find an
equivalent elsewhere. However, fresh or frozen
imported fish of all kinds is increasingly appearing
in fish stores and supermarkets. This chapter contains a
wealth of fish and seafood recipes,
all deliciously satisfying.*

*Most meat in Italy is sold ready boned and
cut across the grain. Veal is a great favorite and
widely available. Pork is also popular, cooked with
lots of fragrant herbs, with roast pig being the
traditional dish of Umbria. Lamb is often served for
special occasions, cooked on a spit or roasted in the oven
with wine, garlic, and herbs. Poultry dishes provide
some of Italy's finest food. Every part of the chicken is
used, the leftovers generally used for making soups.
Turkey, duck, goose, and guinea fowl are also popular,
as is game. Wild rabbit, hare, wild boar, and deer are
also available, especially in Sardinia.*

Celery & Salt Cod Casserole

Salt cod is dried and salted in order to preserve it. It has an unusual flavor, which goes particularly well with celery in this dish.

Serves 4

INGREDIENTS

9 ounces salt cod, soaked overnight
1 tbsp oil
4 shallots, finely chopped
2 garlic cloves, chopped

3 celery stalks, chopped
14 ounce can tomatoes, chopped
$^2/_3$ cup fish stock

$^1/_2$ cup pine nuts
2 tbsp roughly chopped tarragon
2 tbsp capers
crusty bread or mashed potatoes,
   to serve

1 Drain the salt cod, rinse it under plenty of running water, and drain again thoroughly. Remove and discard any skin and bones. Pat the fish dry with paper towels and cut it into chunks.

2 Heat the oil in a large skillet. Add the shallots and garlic and cook for 2–3 minutes. Add the celery and cook for a further 2 minutes, then add the tomatoes and stock.

3 Bring the mixture to a boil, reduce the heat, and simmer for 5 minutes.

4 Add the fish and cook for 10 minutes, or until tender.

5 Meanwhile, spread out the pine nuts on a cookie sheet. Place under a preheated broiler and toast for 2–3 minutes, or until golden.

6 Stir the tarragon, capers, and pine nuts into the fish casserole and heat gently to warm through.

7 Transfer to serving plates and serve with fresh crusty bread or mashed potatoes.

COOK'S TIP

Salt cod is a useful ingredient to have on hand, and once soaked, can be used in the same way as any other fish. It does, however, have a stronger flavor than normal, and it is, of course, slightly salty. It can be found in fish markets, larger supermarkets, and delicatessens.

Salt Cod Fritters

These tasty little fried cakes of mashed salt cod mixed with fennel and a little chili make an excellent snack or main course served with vegetables and a chili relish.

Makes 28 cakes

INGREDIENTS

$3/4$ cup self-rising flour
1 egg, beaten
$2/3$ cup milk
9 ounces salt cod, soaked overnight

1 small red onion, finely chopped
1 small fennel bulb, finely chopped
1 fresh red chili, finely chopped
2 tbsp oil

TO SERVE:
crisp salad, chili relish, cooked rice,
    and fresh vegetables

1 Sift the flour into a large bowl. Make a well in the center of the flour and add the egg.

2 Using a wooden spoon, gradually draw in the flour, slowly adding the milk, and mix to form a smooth batter. Let stand for 10 minutes.

3 Drain the salt cod and rinse it in under running water. Drain again thoroughly.

4 Remove and discard the skin and any bones from the fish, then mash the flesh with a fork.

5 Place the fish in a large bowl and combine with the onion, fennel, and chili. Add the mixture to the batter and blend together.

6 Heat the oil in a large skillet and, taking about 1 tablespoon of the mixture at a time, spoon it into the hot oil. Cook the fritters, in batches, for 3–4 minutes on each side, until golden and slightly puffed. Keep warm while cooking the remaining mixture.

7 Serve with salad and a chili relish for a light meal or with vegetables and rice.

COOK'S TIP

If you prefer larger fritters, use 2 tablespoons per fritter and cook for slightly longer.

Sardinian Red Mullet

Red mullet has a beautiful pink skin, which is enhanced in this dish by being cooked in red wine and orange juice.

Serves 4

INGREDIENTS

¹/₃ cup golden raisins

²/₃ cup red wine

2 tbsp olive oil

2 medium onions, sliced

1 zucchini, cut into
  2-inch sticks

2 oranges

2 tsp coriander seeds, lightly crushed

4 red mullet, filleted

1³/₄ ounce can anchovy fillets,
  drained

2 tbsp chopped, fresh oregano

1 Place the golden raisins in a bowl. Add the red wine and set aside to soak for 10 minutes.

2 Heat the oil in a large skillet. Add the onions and sauté for 2 minutes.

3 Add the zucchini to the skillet and sauté for a further 3 minutes, or until tender.

4 Using a grater, pare long, thin strips from one of the oranges. Using a sharp knife, remove the skin from both of the oranges, then segment them by slicing between the lines of pith.

5 Add the orange zest to the skillet. Add the red wine, golden raisins, coriander seeds, red mullet, and anchovies to the pan and simmer for 10–15 minutes, or until the fish is cooked through.

6 Stir in the oregano and set aside to cool. Place the mixture in a large bowl, cover, and chill in the refrigerator for at least 2 hours to allow the flavors to mingle. Transfer to serving plates and serve.

COOK'S TIP

Red mullet is usually available all year round—frozen, if not fresh—from your fish store or supermarket. If you cannot get ahold of it, try using tilapia. This dish can also be served warm, if you prefer.

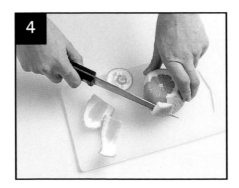

Herring with Hot Pesto Sauce

By making a simple pesto sauce, but omitting the cheese, it is possible to heat the paste without it becoming stringy, so it can be used as a hot sauce.

Serves 4

INGREDIENTS

4 herrings or small mackerel, cleaned and gutted
2 tbsp olive oil

8 ounces tomatoes, peeled, seeded, and chopped
8 canned anchovy fillets, chopped

about 30 fresh basil leaves
1/2 cup pine nuts
2 garlic cloves, crushed

1 Cook the herrings under a preheated broiler for about 8-10 minutes on each side, or until the skin is slightly charred on both sides.

2 Meanwhile, heat 1 tablespoon of the olive oil in a large saucepan.

3 Add the tomatoes and anchovies to the saucepan and cook over a medium heat for 5 minutes.

4 Meanwhile, place the basil, pine nuts, garlic, and remaining oil into a food processor and blend to form a smooth paste. Alternatively, pound the ingredients by hand in a mortar with a pestle.

5 Add the pesto mixture to the saucepan containing the tomato and anchovy mixture, and stir to heat through.

6 Spoon some of the pesto sauce onto warm individual serving plates. Place the fish on top and pour the rest of the pesto sauce over the fish. Serve immediately.

COOK'S TIP

Try barbecuing the fish for an extra charbroiled flavor, if desired.

Broiled Stuffed Sole

*A delicious stuffing of sun-dried tomatoes and fresh lemon
thyme are used to stuff whole sole.*

Serves 4

INGREDIENTS

1 tbsp olive oil

2 tbsp butter

1 small onion, finely chopped

1 garlic clove, chopped

3 sun-dried tomatoes, chopped

2 tbsp lemon thyme

1 cup bread crumbs

1 tbsp lemon juice

4 small sole, gutted and cleaned

salt and pepper

lemon wedges, to garnish

fresh salad greens, to serve

1 Heat the oil and butter in a skillet until it is just beginning to froth.

2 Add the onion and garlic to the skillet and cook, stirring, for 5 minutes, until just softened.

3 To make the stuffing, mix the tomatoes, thyme, bread crumbs, and lemon juice in a bowl, and season to taste.

4 Add the stuffing mixture to the skillet and stir well to mix.

5 Using a sharp knife, pare the skin from the bone inside the slit of the fish to make a pocket. Spoon the tomato and herb stuffing into the pocket.

6 Cook the fish under a preheated broiler for 6 minutes on each side, or until golden brown.

7 Transfer the stuffed fish to warm serving plates and garnish with lemon wedges. Serve immediately with fresh salad greens.

COOK'S TIP

*Lemon thyme has a delicate lemon
scent and flavor. Ordinary thyme
can be used instead, but mix it with
1 teaspoon lemon rind to add
extra flavor.*

Sole Fillets in Marsala & Cream

A rich wine and cream sauce makes this an excellent dinner party dish. You can make the stock the day before, so it takes only minutes to cook and serve the fish.

Serves 4

INGREDIENTS

STOCK:
2^1/$_2$ cups water
bones and skin from the sole fillets
1 onion, peeled and halved
1 carrot, peeled and halved
3 fresh bay leaves

SAUCE:
1 tbsp olive oil
1 tbsp butter
4 shallots, finely chopped
3^1/$_2$ ounces baby button mushrooms,
  wiped and halved

1 tbsp peppercorns, lightly crushed
8 sole fillets
^{1}/$_3$ cup Marsala
^{2}/$_3$ pint heavy cream

1 To make the stock, place the water, fish bones and skin, onion, carrot, and bay leaves in a saucepan and bring to a boil.

2 Reduce the heat and simmer the mixture for 1 hour, or until the stock has reduced to about ^{2}/$_3$ cup. Drain the stock through a fine strainer, discarding the bones and vegetables, and set aside.

3 To make the sauce, heat the oil and butter in a skillet. Add the shallots and cook, stirring occasionally, for 2–3 minutes, or until just softened.

4 Add the mushrooms to the skillet and cook, stirring occasionally, for a further 2–3 minutes, or until they are just beginning to brown.

5 Add the peppercorns and sole fillets to the skillet. Fry the sole fillets for 3–4 minutes on each side, or until a golden brown color.

6 Pour the wine and stock over the fish and simmer for 3 minutes. Remove the fish with a fish slice or a slotted spoon, set aside, and keep warm.

7 Increase the heat and boil the mixture in the skillet for about 5 minutes, or until the sauce has reduced and thickened.

8 Pour in the cream, return the fish to the skillet, and heat through. Serve with cooked vegetables of your choice.

Fresh Baked Sardines

Here, fresh sardines are baked with eggs, herbs, and vegetables to form a dish similar to an omelet.

Serves 4

INGREDIENTS

2 tbsp olive oil

2 large onions, sliced into rings

3 garlic cloves, chopped

2 large zucchini, cut into sticks

3 tbsp fresh thyme, stalks removed

8 sardine fillets or about 2^1/4 pounds sardines, filleted

1 cup grated Parmesan cheese

4 eggs, beaten

^{2}/3 pint milk

salt and pepper

1 Heat 1 tablespoon of the olive oil in a skillet. Add the onion rings and chopped garlic and sauté for about 2–3 minutes.

2 Add the zucchini to the skillet and cook, stirring occasionally, for about 5 minutes, or until golden.

3 Stir 2 tablespoons of the thyme into the mixture.

4 Place half the onions and zucchini in the base of a large ovenproof dish. Top with the sardine fillets and half the grated Parmesan cheese.

5 Place the remaining onions and zucchini on top and sprinkle with the remaining thyme.

6 Mix the eggs and milk together in a bowl and season to taste with salt and pepper. Pour the mixture over the vegetables and sardines in the dish. Sprinkle the remaining Parmesan cheese over the top.

7 Bake in a preheated oven at 350°F for 20–25 minutes, or until golden and set. Serve the fresh baked sardines hot, straight from the oven.

VARIATION

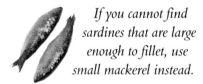

If you cannot find sardines that are large enough to fillet, use small mackerel instead.

Marinated Fish

Marinating fish, for even a short period, adds a subtle flavor to the flesh and makes even simply broiled or fried fish a delicious dish.

Serves 4

INGREDIENTS

4 mackerel
4 tbsp chopped marjoram

2 tbsp extra-virgin olive oil
finely grated rind and juice of 1 lime

2 garlic cloves, crushed
salt and pepper

1 Under gently running water, scrape the mackerel with the blunt side of a knife to remove any scales.

2 Using a sharp knife, make a slit in the stomach of the fish and cut horizontally along until the knife will go no farther very easily. Gut the fish and rinse under water. You may prefer to remove the heads before cooking, but it is not necessary.

3 Using a sharp knife, cut 4–5 diagonal slashes on each side of the fish. Place the fish in a shallow, nonmetallic dish.

4 To make the marinade, mix together the marjoram, olive oil, lime rind and juice, garlic, and salt and pepper in a bowl.

5 Pour the mixture over the fish. Marinate in the refrigerator for 30 minutes.

6 Cook the mackerel, under a preheated broiler, for 5–6 minutes on each side, brushing occasionally with the reserved marinade, until golden.

7 Transfer the fish to serving plates. Pour over any remaining marinade before serving.

COOK'S TIP

If the lime is too hard to squeeze, microwave on high for 30 seconds to release the juice. This dish is also excellent cooked on the grill.

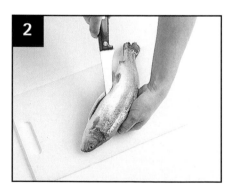

Orange Mackerel

Mackerel can be quite rich, but when it is stuffed with oranges and toasted ground almonds it is tangy and light.

Serves 4

INGREDIENTS

2 tbsp oil
4 scallions, chopped
2 oranges
1/2 cup ground almonds

1 tbsp oats
1/2 cup pitted mixed green and black olives, chopped

8 mackerel fillets
salt and pepper
crisp salad greens, to serve

1 Heat the oil in a skillet. Add the scallions, stirring occasionally, and cook for about 2 minutes.

2 Finely grate the rind of the oranges, then, using a sharp knife, cut away the remaining skin and white pith.

3 Using a sharp knife, segment the oranges by cutting down either side of the lines of pith to loosen each segment. Do this over a plate so that you can reserve any juice. Cut each orange segment in half.

4 Lightly toast the almonds, under a preheated broiler, for 2–3 minutes, or until golden; watch them carefully as they brown very quickly.

5 Mix the scallions, oranges, any juice, the ground almonds, oats, and olives together in a bowl and season to taste with salt and pepper.

6 Spoon the orange mixture along the center of each mackerel fillet. Roll up each mackerel fillet, securing it in place with a toothpick.

7 Bake in a preheated oven at 375°F for 25 minutes, until the fish is tender.

8 Transfer to serving plates and serve warm with salad greens.

Italian Cod

Cod roasted with herbs and topped with a lemon and rosemary crust is a delicious main course.

Serves 4

INGREDIENTS

2 tbsp butter
2 cups whole-wheat bread crumbs
$1/4$ cup chopped walnuts
grated rind and juice of 2 lemons

2 sprigs rosemary, stalks removed
2 tbsp chopped parsley
4 cod fillets, each about $5^1/_2$ oz

1 garlic clove, crushed
3 tbsp walnut oil
1 small fresh red chili, diced
salad greens, to serve

1 Melt the butter in a large skillet.

2 Remove the skillet from the heat and add the bread crumbs, walnuts, the rind and juice of 1 lemon, half the rosemary, and half the parsley.

3 Arrange the cod fillets in a single layer in a shallow, foil-lined roasting pan. Press the bread crumb mixture over the top of the cod fillets.

4 Bake in a preheated oven at 400°F for 25–30 minutes, or until tender.

5 Mix the garlic, the remaining lemon rind and juice, rosemary, parsley, and chili in a bowl. Beat in the walnut oil and mix to combine. Drizzle the dressing over the cod fillets as soon as they are cooked.

6 Transfer to serving plates and serve immediately.

VARIATION

If desired, the walnuts may be omitted from the crust. In addition, extra-virgin olive oil can be used instead of walnut oil, if you prefer.

COOK'S TIP

The "hotness" of chilies varies, so use them with caution. As a general guide, the smaller the chili the hotter it will be.

Mussel Casserole

Mussels are not difficult to cook, just a little messy to eat. The flavors are worth it, however, and serving this dish with a finger bowl helps to keep things clean!

Serves 4

INGREDIENTS

$2^{1}/_{4}$ pounds mussels
$^{2}/_{3}$ cup white wine
1 tbsp oil

1 onion, finely chopped
3 garlic cloves, chopped
1 red chili, finely chopped

$3^{1}/_{2}$ ounces tomato sauce
1 tbsp chopped marjoram
toast or crusty bread, to serve

1 Scrub the mussels to remove any mud or sand.

2 Remove the beards from the mussels by pulling away the hairy protrusion between the two shells. Rinse the mussels in a bowl of clean water. Discard any mussels that do not close when they are tapped—they are dead and should not be eaten.

3 Place the mussels in a large saucepan. Pour in the wine and cook for 5 minutes, shaking the pan occasionally until the shells open. Remove and discard any mussels that do not open.

4 Remove the mussels from the saucepan with a slotted spoon. Strain the cooking liquid through a fine strainer set over a bowl, reserving the cooking liquid.

5 Heat the oil in a large skillet. Add the onion, garlic, and chili and cook for 4–5 minutes, or until softened.

6 Add the reserved cooking liquid to the pan and cook for 5 minutes, or until reduced.

7 Stir in the tomato sauce, marjoram, and mussels and cook until hot.

8 Transfer to serving bowls and serve with toast or plenty of crusty bread to mop up the juices.

COOK'S TIP

Finger bowls are individual bowls of warm water with a slice of lemon floating in them. They are used to clean your fingers at the end of a meal.

Stuffed Squid

*Whole squid are stuffed with a mixture of fresh herbs and
sun-dried tomatoes and then cooked in a wine sauce.*

Serves 4

INGREDIENTS

8 prepared whole squid
6 canned anchovies, chopped
2 garlic cloves, chopped

2 tbsp rosemary, stalks removed and
  leaves chopped
2 sun-dried tomatoes, chopped
3 cups bread crumbs
1 tbsp olive oil

1 onion, finely chopped
3/4 cup white wine
3/4 cup fish stock
cooked rice, to serve

1 Remove the tentacles from the body of the squid and chop the flesh finely.

2 Grind the anchovies, garlic, rosemary, and tomatoes to a paste in a mortar with a pestle.

3 Add the bread crumbs and the chopped squid tentacles and mix. If the mixture is too dry to form a thick paste at this point, add 1 teaspoon water.

4 Spoon the paste into the body sacs of the squid, then tie a length of cotton around the end of each sac to fasten them. Do not overfill the sacs, because they will expand during cooking.

5 Heat the oil in a skillet. Add the onion and sauté, stirring, for 3–4 minutes, or until golden.

6 Add the stuffed squid to the skillet and cook for 3–4 minutes, or until golden brown all over.

7 Add the wine and stock and bring to a boil. Reduce the heat, cover, and then simmer for 15 minutes.

8 Remove the lid and cook for a further 5 minutes, until the squid is tender and the juices have reduced. Serve with cooked rice.

COOK'S TIP

*If you cannot buy whole squid, use
squid pieces and stir the paste into
the sauce with the wine and stock.*

Rich Beef Stew

This slow-cooked beef stew is flavored with oranges, red wine, and porcini mushrooms.

Serves 4

INGREDIENTS

1 tbsp oil
1 tbsp butter
8 ounces baby onions, peeled
  and halved

1¼ pounds stewing steak, diced into
  1½-inch chunks
1¼ cups beef stock
²⁄₃ cup red wine
4 tbsp chopped oregano
1 tbsp sugar

1 orange
1 ounce porcini or other dried
  mushrooms
8 ounces fresh plum tomatoes
cooked rice or potatoes, to serve

1 Heat the oil and butter in a large skillet. Add the baby onions and sauté for 5 minutes, or until golden. Remove with a slotted spoon, set aside, and keep warm.

2 Add the beef to the skillet and cook, stirring, for 5 minutes, or until browned all over.

3 Return the onions to the skillet and add the stock, wine, oregano, and sugar, stirring to mix thoroughly. Transfer the mixture to an ovenproof casserole dish.

4 Pare the rind from the orange and cut it into strips. Slice the orange flesh into rings. Add the orange rings and the rind to the casserole. Cook in a preheated oven at 350°F for 1¼ hours.

5 Soak the porcini mushrooms for 30 minutes in a small bowl containing 4 tablespoons warm water.

6 Skin and halve the tomatoes. Add the tomatoes, porcini mushrooms, and their soaking liquid to the casserole. Cook for a further 20 minutes, until the beef

is tender and the juices thickened. Serve with cooked rice or potatoes.

VARIATION

Instead of fresh tomatoes, try using 8 sun-dried tomatoes, cut into wide strips.

Pork with Lemon & Garlic

This is a simplified version of a traditional dish from the Marche region, on the east coast of Italy. Pork tenderloin pockets are stuffed with prosciutto and herbs.

Serves 4

INGREDIENTS

1 pound pork tenderloin
1/2 cup chopped almonds
2 tbsp olive oil
2/3 cup finely chopped prosciutto

2 garlic cloves, chopped
1 tbsp fresh oregano, chopped
finely grated rind of 2 lemons
4 shallots, finely chopped

3/4 cup ham or chicken stock
1 tsp sugar

1 Using a sharp knife, cut the pork tenderloin into 4 equal pieces. Place them between sheets of wax paper and pound each piece with a meat mallet or the end of a rolling pin to flatten it.

2 Cut a horizontal slit in each piece of pork to make a pocket.

3 Spread out the almonds on a cookie sheet. Lightly toast the almonds under a preheated broiler for 2–3 minutes, or until golden brown.

4 Mix the almonds with 1 tablespoon of the olive oil, the prosciutto, garlic, oregano, and the finely grated rind from 1 lemon. Carefully spoon the mixture into the pockets of the pork.

5 Heat the remaining olive oil in a large skillet. Add the chopped shallots and sauté for 2 minutes.

6 Add the pork to the skillet and cook for 2 minutes on each side or until browned all over.

7 Add the stock to the skillet, bring to a boil, cover, and simmer for 45 minutes, or until the pork is tender. Remove the meat from the skillet, set aside, and keep warm.

8 Using a grater, pare the remaining lemon. Add the rind and sugar to the pan and boil for 3–4 minutes, or until reduced and syrupy. Pour over the pork tenderloin and serve immediately.

Porkchops with Fennel & Juniper

*The addition of juniper and fennel to the porkchops gives
an unusual and delicate flavor to this dish.*

Serves 4

INGREDIENTS

$^1/_2$ fennel bulb
1 tbsp juniper berries, lightly crushed
about 2 tbsp olive oil

finely grated rind and juice of
  1 orange

4 porkchops, each about 5$^1/_2$ oz
fresh bread and a crisp salad, to serve

1 Using a sharp knife, finely chop the fennel bulb, discarding the green parts.

2 Grind the juniper berries in a mortar with a pestle. Mix the crushed juniper berries with the fennel flesh, olive oil, and orange rind.

3 Using a sharp knife, score a few cuts all over each chop.

4 Place the porkchops in a single layer in a roasting pan or an ovenproof dish. Spoon the fennel and juniper mixture over the porkchops.

5 Carefully pour the orange juice over the top of each porkchop, cover, and marinate in the refrigerator for about 2 hours.

6 Drain the porkchops and cook under a preheated broiler, for 10–15 minutes, depending on the thickness of the meat, until the pork is tender and cooked through, turning occasionally.

7 Transfer the porkchops to serving plates and serve with a crisp, fresh salad and plenty of fresh bread to mop up the cooking juices.

COOK'S TIP

Juniper berries are most commonly associated with gin, but they are often added to meat dishes in Italy for a delicate citrus flavor. They can be bought dried from most health food shops and supermarkets.

Pork Cooked in Milk

*This traditional dish of boneless pork cooked with garlic
and milk can be served hot or cold.*

Serves 4

INGREDIENTS

1 pound 12 ounces boneless leg
  of pork
1 tbsp oil
2 tbsp butter
1 onion, chopped

2 garlic cloves, chopped
$\frac{1}{2}$ cup diced pancetta
5 cups milk
1 tbsp green peppercorns, crushed

2 fresh bay leaves
2 tbsp marjoram
2 tbsp thyme

1 Using a sharp knife, remove the fat from the pork. Shape the meat into a neat form, tying it in place with a length of string.

2 Heat the oil and butter in a large saucepan. Add the onion, garlic, and pancetta to the pan and cook for 2–3 minutes.

3 Add the pork to the pan and cook, turning occasionally, until it is browned all over.

4 Pour the milk in, add the peppercorns, bay leaves, marjoram, and thyme, and cook over a low heat for 1¼–1½ hours, or until tender. Watch the liquid carefully for the last 15 minutes of the cooking time because it tends to reduce very quickly and will then burn. If the liquid reduces and the pork is still not tender, add another ½ cup milk and continue cooking. Reserve the cooking liquid.

5 Remove the pork from the saucepan. Using a sharp knife, cut the meat into slices. Transfer the pork slices to serving plates and serve immediately with the sauce (see Cook's Tip).

COOK'S TIP

As the milk reduces naturally in this dish, it forms a thick and creamy sauce, which curdles slightly but tastes delicious.

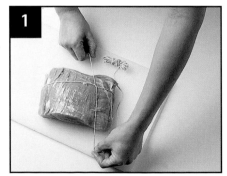

Neapolitan Porkchops

An Italian version of broiled porkchops, this dish is easy to make and delicious to eat.

Serves 4

INGREDIENTS

2 tbsp olive oil
1 garlic clove, chopped
1 large onion, sliced
14 ounce can tomatoes

2 tsp yeast extract
4 pork loin chops, each about
  $4^1/_2$ oz
$^3/_4$ cup pitted black olives

2 tbsp fresh basil, shredded
freshly grated Parmesan cheese,
  to serve

1 Heat the oil in a large skillet. Add the onions and garlic and sauté for 3–4 minutes, or until the onions are just beginning to soften.

2 Add the tomatoes and yeast extract to the skillet and simmer for about 5 minutes, or until the sauce just starts to thicken.

3 Cook the porkchops under a preheated broiler for 5 minutes on both sides, until the the meat is golden and cooked through. Set the porkchops aside and keep warm.

4 Add the olives and fresh shredded basil to the sauce in the skillet and stir quickly to combine.

5 Transfer the chops to warm serving plates. Top with the sauce, sprinkle with freshly grated Parmesan cheese, and serve immediately.

COOK'S TIP

Parmesan is a mature and exceptionally hard cheese produced in Italy. You need to add only a little, as it has a very strong flavor.

COOK'S TIP

There are many types of canned tomato available—for example plum tomatoes, or chopped tomatoes in water, or chopped sieved tomatoes (passata). The chopped variety are often canned with added flavors, such as garlic, basil, onion, chili, and mixed herbs, and are a good standby.

Roman Pan-fried Lamb

Chunks of tender lamb, pan-fried with garlic and stewed in red wine, make a real Roman dish.

Serves 4

INGREDIENTS

1 tbsp oil
1 tbsp butter
1¼ pounds lamb (shoulder or leg), cut in 1-inch cubes
4 garlic cloves, peeled

3 sprigs thyme, stalks removed
6 canned anchovy fillets
²/₃ cup red wine
²/₃ cup lamb or vegetable stock

1 tsp sugar
½ cup pitted black olives, halved
2 tbsp chopped parsley, to garnish
mashed potato, to serve

1 Heat the oil and butter in a large skillet. Add the cubes of lamb and cook for 4–5 minutes, stirring, until the meat is browned all over.

2 Using a pestle and mortar, grind together the garlic, thyme, and anchovies to make a smooth paste.

3 Add the wine and lamb or vegetable stock to the skillet, stirring to mix. Stir in the garlic and anchovy paste, together with the sugar.

4 Bring the mixture to a boil, reduce the heat, cover and simmer for 30–40 minutes, or until the lamb is tender. For the last 10 minutes of the cooking time, remove the lid in order to allow the sauce to reduce slightly.

5 Stir the olives into the sauce and mix to combine.

6 Transfer the lamb and the sauce to a serving dish and garnish with freshly chopped parsley. Serve with creamy mashed potatoes.

COOK'S TIP

Rome is the capital of both the region of Lazio and Italy and thus has become a focal point for specialties from all over Italy. Food from this region tends to be fairly simple and quick to prepare, all with plenty of herbs and seasonings giving really robust flavors.

Lamb Noisettes with Lemon

These lamb chops quickly become more elegant when the bone is removed to make noisettes.

Serves 4

INGREDIENTS

4 lamb chops
1 tbsp oil
1 tbsp butter

$2/3$ cup white wine
$2/3$ cup lamb or vegetable stock

2 bay leaves
pared rind of 1 lemon
salt and pepper

1 Using a sharp knife, carefully remove the bone from each lamb chop, keeping the meat intact. Alternatively, ask your butcher to prepare the lamb noisettes for you.

2 Shape the meat into rounds and secure with a length of string.

3 In a large skillet, heat together the oil and butter until the mixture is just beginning to froth. Add the lamb noisettes to the skillet and cook for 2–3 minutes on each side, or until browned all over.

4 Remove the skillet from the heat, drain off all of the fat, and discard.

5 Return the skillet to the heat. Add the wine, stock, bay leaves, and lemon rind to the skillet and cook over a medium heat for 20–25 minutes, or until the lamb is tender.

6 Season the lamb noisettes and sauce to taste with a little salt and pepper.

7 Transfer to serving plates. Remove the string and serve the noisettes with the sauce.

COOK'S TIP

Your local butcher will offer you good advice on how to prepare the lamb noisettes, if you are wary of preparing them yourself.

Chicken Marengo

Napoleon's chef was ordered to cook a sumptuous meal on the eve of the battle of Marengo.
He gathered everything possible to make a feast, and this was the result.

Serves 4

INGREDIENTS

1 tbsp olive oil
8 chicken pieces
10$^{1}/_{2}$ ounces tomato sauce
$^{3}/_{4}$ cup white wine
2 tsp dried mixed herbs
8 slices white bread

3 tbsp butter, melted
2 garlic cloves, crushed
3$^{1}/_{2}$ ounces mixed mushrooms (such
as button, oyster, and ceps)

$^{1}/_{2}$ cup pitted black olives, chopped
1 tsp sugar
fresh basil, to garnish

1 Using a sharp knife, remove the bone from each of the chicken pieces.

2 Heat the oil in a large skillet. Add the chicken pieces and cook, turning occasionally, for 4–5 minutes, or until browned all over.

3 Add the tomato sauce, wine, and mixed herbs to the skillet. Bring to a boil and then simmer for 30 minutes, or until the chicken is tender and the juices run clear when a toothpick is inserted into the thickest part of the meat.

4 Mix the melted butter and crushed garlic together. Lightly toast the slices of bread and brush with the garlic butter.

5 Add the remaining oil to a separate skillet and cook the mushrooms for 2–3 minutes, or until just brown.

6 Add the olives and sugar to the chicken mixture and warm through.

7 Transfer the chicken and sauce to serving plates. Serve with the bruschetta (fried bread) and fried mushrooms.

COOK'S TIP

If you have time, marinate the chicken pieces in the wine and herbs in the refrigerator for 2 hours. This will make the chicken more tender and accentuate the wine flavor of the sauce.

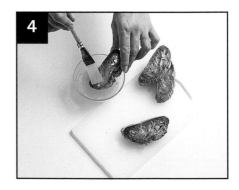

Prosciutto-wrapped Chicken

There is a delicious surprise inside these chicken breast packets!

Serves 4

INGREDIENTS

4 skinless chicken breasts
$^1/_2$ cup cream cheese, flavored with
  herbs and garlic

8 slices prosciutto
$^2/_3$ cup red wine

$^2/_3$ cup chicken stock
1 tbsp brown sugar

1 Using a sharp knife, make a horizontal slit along the length of each chicken breast to form a pocket.

2 Beat the cheese with a wooden spoon to soften it. Spoon the cheese into the pocket of the chicken breasts.

3 Wrap 2 slices of prosciutto around each chicken breast and secure in place with a length of string.

4 Pour the wine and chicken stock into a large skillet and bring to a boil over a medium heat. When the mixture is just starting to boil, add the sugar and stir to dissolve.

5 Add the chicken breasts to the skillet. Lower the heat and simmer for about 12–15 minutes, or until the chicken is tender and the juices run clear when a toothpick is inserted into the thickest part of the meat.

6 Remove the chicken from the pan, set aside, and keep warm.

7 Reheat the sauce and boil until reduced and thickened. Remove the string and cut the chicken into slices. Pour the sauce over the chicken to serve.

VARIATION

Try adding 2 finely chopped sun-dried tomatoes to the soft cheese in step 2, if desired.

Chicken with Balsamic Vinegar

*A rich caramelized sauce, flavored with balsamic vinegar and wine,
gives this chicken dish a piquant flavor.*

Serves 4

INGREDIENTS

4 boneless chicken thighs	1 tbsp oil	2 tbsp fresh thyme
2 garlic cloves, crushed	1 tbsp butter	salt and pepper
3/4 cup red wine	4 shallots	cooked polenta or rice, to serve
3 tbsp white wine vinegar	3 tbsp balsamic vinegar	

1 Using a sharp knife, make a few slashes in the skin of the chicken. Brush the chicken with the crushed garlic and place in a nonmetallic dish.

2 Pour the wine and white wine vinegar over the chicken and season to taste with a little salt and pepper. Cover and marinate in the refrigerator, preferably overnight.

3 Carefully remove the chicken pieces with a slotted spoon, draining well, and reserve the marinade.

4 Heat the oil and butter in a skillet. Add the shallots and sauté for 2–3 minutes, or until they begin to soften.

5 Add the chicken pieces to the skillet and cook for about 3-4 minutes, turning, until browned all over. Reduce the heat and add half the reserved marinade. Cover and cook for 15–20 minutes, adding more marinade when necessary.

6 Add the balsamic vinegar and thyme and cook for a further 4 minutes.

7 Transfer the chicken and marinade to serving plates and serve with polenta or rice.

COOK'S TIP

To make the chicken pieces look a little neater, use toothpicks to hold them together or secure them with a length of string.

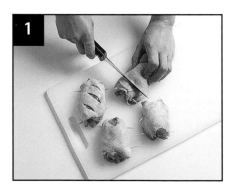

Saltimbocca

The Italian name for this dish, Saltimbocca, *means "jump into the mouth." The stuffed rolls are quick and easy to make and taste delicious.*

Serves 4

INGREDIENTS

4 turkey fillets or 4 veal escalopes, about 1 pound in total
3 3/4 ounces prosciutto

8 sage leaves
1 tbsp olive oil
1 onion, finely chopped

3/4 cup white wine
3/4 cup chicken stock

1 Place the turkey or veal between sheets of wax paper. Pound the meat with a meat mallet or the end of a rolling pin to flatten it slightly. Cut each escalope in half.

2 Trim the prosciutto to fit each piece of turkey or veal and place over the meat. Lay a sage leaf on top. Roll up the escalopes and secure with a toothpick.

3 Heat the oil in a skillet and sauté the onion for 3–4 minutes. Add the turkey or veal rolls to the skillet and cook for 5 minutes, until golden brown all over.

4 Pour the wine and stock into the skillet and simmer for 15 minutes if using turkey, and 20 minutes for veal, or until tender. Serve immediately.

VARIATION

Try a similar recipe called Bocconcini, *meaning "little mouthfuls." Follow the same method as here, but replace the sage leaf with a piece of Swiss cheese.*

COOK'S TIP

If using turkey rather than veal, watch it carefully, as turkey tends to turn dry very quickly if overcooked.

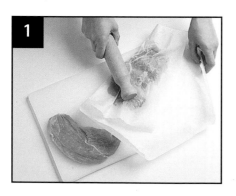

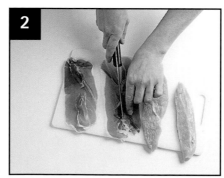

Escalopes with Italian Sausage & Capers

Anchovies are often used to enhance flavor, particularly in meat dishes.
Either veal or turkey escalopes can be used for this pan-fried dish.

Serves 4

INGREDIENTS

1 tbsp olive oil
6 canned anchovy fillets, drained
1 tbsp capers, drained
1 tbsp fresh rosemary, stalks removed

finely grated rind and juice of
   1 orange
$^3/_4$ cup diced Italian sausage
3 tomatoes, skinned and chopped

4 turkey or veal escalopes, each
   about $4^1/_2$ oz
salt and pepper
crusty bread or cooked polenta,
   to serve

1 Heat the oil in a large skillet. Add the anchovies, capers, fresh rosemary, orange rind and juice, Italian sausage, and tomatoes and cook for about 5–6 minutes, stirring occasionally.

2 Meanwhile, place the turkey or veal escalopes between sheets of wax paper. Pound the meat with a meat mallet or the end of a rolling pin to flatten it.

3 Add the meat to the mixture in the skillet. Season to taste with salt and pepper, cover, and cook for 3–5 minutes on each side, or slightly longer if the meat is thicker.

4 Transfer to serving plates and serve with fresh crusty bread or cooked polenta.

VARIATION

Try using 4-minute steaks, slightly flattened, instead of the turkey or veal. Cook them for 4–5 minutes on top of the sauce in the skillet.

COOK'S TIP

Polenta is typical of northern Italian cuisine. It is often fried or toasted and used to mop up the juices of the main course.

Italian Sausage & Bean Casserole

*In this traditional Tuscan dish, Italian sausages are cooked
with cannellini beans and tomatoes.*

Serves 4

INGREDIENTS

8 Italian sausages
1 tbsp olive oil
1 large onion, chopped
2 garlic cloves, chopped

1 green bell pepper
8 ounces fresh tomatoes, skinned
  and chopped or 14 ounce can
  tomatoes, chopped

2 tbsp sun-dried tomato paste
14 ounce can cannellini beans
mashed potato or rice, to serve

1 Seed the bell pepper and cut it into thin strips.

2 Prick the Italian sausages all over with a fork. Cook them, under a preheated broiler for 10–12 minutes, turning occasionally, until brown all over. Set aside and keep warm.

3 Heat the oil in a large skillet. Add the onion, garlic, and bell pepper strips to the skillet and cook for 5 minutes, stirring occasionally, or until the onion has softened.

4 Add the tomatoes to the skillet and simmer the mixture over a medium heat, stirring occasionally, for about 5 minutes, or until slightly reduced and thickened.

5 Stir the sun-dried tomato paste, cannellini beans, and Italian sausages into the mixture in the skillet. Cook for about 4–5 minutes, or until the mixture is piping hot. Add 4–5 tablespoons of water, stirring well, if the mixture becomes too dry during cooking.

6 Transfer the Italian sausage and bean casserole to serving plates and serve with mashed potato or cooked rice.

COOK'S TIP

Italian sausages are coarse in texture and have quite a strong flavor. They can be found in specialty sausage shops, Italian delicatessens, and some supermarkets. Game sausages are the only substitutes in this recipe.

Pizzas & Breads

There is little to beat the irresistible aroma and taste of a freshly made pizza cooked in a wood-fired brick oven. However, a homemade dough base and a freshly made tomato sauce will give you the closest thing possible to an authentic Italian pizza. Pizzas can have every imaginable type of topping. There are endless varieties of salamis and cured meats, hams and sausages, which all make excellent toppings. Canned or fresh fish or seafood are also good. Vegetables of all kinds make the most tempting and attractive pizza toppings. Choose the best quality vegetables and herbs for maximum flavor. A variety of antipasti, such as artichoke hearts, sun-dried tomatoes, sliced bell peppers, and mushrooms, are sold in jars of olive oil and these make the most delicious and convenient toppings. You can also use the oil from the jar to drizzle over the pizza before baking to keep it moist.

There is nothing quite like the smell of freshly baked bread, and the Italians do it so well. They combine the sun-drenched flavors of the Mediterranean with delicious fresh and crusty bread—a winning combination. You can use the breads in this chapter to mop up the delicious juices from a range of Italian dishes, or you can eat them on their own as a tasty snack.

Pizza Margherita

Pizza means "pie" in Italian. The fresh bread dough is not difficult
to make, but it does take a little time.

Serves 4

INGREDIENTS

BASIC PIZZA DOUGH:
$1/4$ ounce dried yeast
1 tsp sugar
1 cup lukewarm water
12 ounces strong flour
1 tsp salt
1 tbsp olive oil

TOPPING:
14 ounce can tomatoes, chopped
2 garlic cloves, crushed
2 tsp dried basil
1 tbsp olive oil
2 tbsp tomato paste
$3^1/2$ ounces mozzarella cheese, diced

2 tbsp freshly grated Parmesan
cheese
salt and pepper

1 Place the yeast and sugar in a bowl and mix with 4 tbsp of the water. Set the yeast mixture aside in a warm place for 15 minutes, or until frothy.

2 Mix the flour with the salt and make a well in the center. Add the oil, the yeast mixture, and the remaining water. Using a wooden spoon, mix to form a dough.

3 Turn the dough out onto a floured surface and knead for 4–5 minutes, or until smooth.

4 Return the dough to the bowl, cover with an oiled sheet of plastic wrap, and leave to rise for 30 minutes, or until doubled in size.

5 Knead the dough for 2 minutes. Stretch the dough with your hands, then place it on a greased cookie sheet, pushing out the edges until even and to the shape required. The dough should be no more than about $1/4$ inch thick because it will rise during cooking.

6 To make the topping, place the tomatoes, garlic, dried basil, olive oil, and salt and pepper to taste in a large skillet and simmer for 20 minutes, or until the sauce has thickened. Stir in the tomato paste and cool slightly.

7 Spread the topping evenly over the pizza base. Top with the mozzarella and Parmesan cheeses and bake in a preheated oven at 400°F for 20–25 minutes. Serve hot.

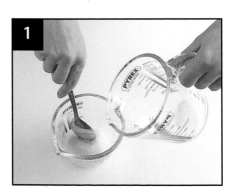

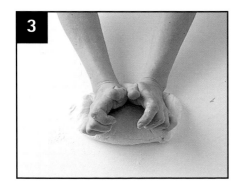

Gorgonzola Pizza

An unusual combination of blue Gorgonzola cheese and pears combine to give a colorful pizza.
The whole-wheat base adds a nutty flavor and texture.

Serves 4

INGREDIENTS

PIZZA DOUGH:
$1/4$ ounce dried yeast
1 tsp sugar
1 cup lukewarm water
$1^1/_2$ cups whole-wheat flour
$1^1/_2$ cups strong white flour

1 tsp salt
1 tbsp olive oil

TOPPING:
3 cups peeled and diced pumpkin
   or squash

1 tbsp olive oil
1 pear, cored, peeled, and sliced
1 cup crumbled Gorgonzola cheese
1 sprig fresh rosemary, to garnish

1 Place the yeast and sugar in a bowl and mix with 4 tbsp of the water. Set the yeast mixture aside in a warm place for 15 minutes, or until frothy.

2 Mix both of the flours with the salt and make a well in the center. Add the oil, the yeast mixture, and the remaining water. Using a wooden spoon, mix to form a dough.

3 Turn the dough out onto a floured surface and knead for 4–5 minutes, or until smooth.

4 Return the dough to the bowl, cover with an oiled sheet of plastic wrap, and set aside to rise for 30 minutes, or until doubled in size.

5 Remove the dough from the bowl. Knead the dough for 2 minutes. Using a rolling pin, roll out the dough to form a long oval shape, then place it on a greased cookie sheet, pushing out the edges until even. The dough should be no more than $1/4$ inch thick because it will rise during cooking.

6 To make the topping, place the pumpkin in a shallow roasting pan. Drizzle with the olive oil and cook under a preheated broiler for 20 minutes, or until soft and lightly golden.

7 Top the dough with the pear and the pumpkin, brushing with the oil from the pan. Sprinkle the Gorgonzola cheese over the top. Bake in a preheated oven, at 400°F for 15 minutes, or until the base is golden. Garnish with a sprig of rosemary.

Onion, Ham, & Cheese Pizza

This pizza was a favorite of the Romans. It is slightly unusual because the topping is made without a tomato sauce base.

Serves 4

INGREDIENTS

1 portion of Basic Pizza Dough (see page 196)

TOPPING:
2 tbsp olive oil
9 ounces onions, sliced into rings
2 garlic cloves, crushed
1 red bell pepper, diced

3^1/$_2$ ounces prosciutto, cut into strips
3^1/$_2$ ounces mozzarella cheese, sliced
2 tbsp rosemary, stalks removed and roughly chopped

1 Place the yeast and sugar in a bowl and mix with 4 tbsp of the water. Set the yeast mixture aside in a warm place for 15 minutes, or until frothy.

2 Mix the flour with the salt and make a well in the center. Add the oil, the yeast mixture, and the remaining water. Using a wooden spoon, mix to form a dough.

3 Turn the dough out onto a floured surface and knead for 4–5 minutes, or until smooth. Return the dough to the bowl, cover with an oiled sheet of plastic wrap, and set aside to rise for 30 minutes, or until doubled in size.

4 Remove the dough from the bowl. Knead the dough for 2 minutes. Using a rolling pin, roll out the dough to form a square shape, then place it on a greased cookie sheet, pushing out the edges until even. The dough should be no more than ^{1}/$_4$ inch thick because it will rise during cooking.

5 To make the topping, heat the oil in a skillet. Add the sliced onions and garlic and sauté for 3 minutes. Add the diced bell pepper and sauté for a further 2 minutes.

6 Cover the skillet and cook the vegetables over a low heat for 10 minutes, stirring occasionally, until the onions are slightly caramelized. Cool slightly.

7 Spread the topping evenly over the pizza base. Place strips of prosciutto, mozzarella, and rosemary over the top. Bake in a preheated oven at 400°F for 20–25 minutes. Serve hot.

Sun-dried Tomatoes & Ricotta Pizza

This is a traditional dish from the Calabrian Mountains in southern Italy, where it is made with naturally sun-dried tomatoes and ricotta cheese.

Serves 4

INGREDIENTS

1 portion Basic Pizza Dough (see page 196)

TOPPING:
4 tbsp sun-dried tomato paste
³/4 cup ricotta cheese

10 sun-dried tomatoes
1 tbsp fresh thyme
salt and pepper

1 Place the yeast and sugar in a bowl and mix with 4 tbsp of the water. Set the yeast mixture aside in a warm place for 15 minutes, or until frothy.

2 Mix the flour with the salt and make a well in the center. Add the oil, the yeast mixture, and the remaining water. Using a wooden spoon, mix to form a dough.

3 Turn the dough out onto a floured surface and knead for 4–5 minutes, or until smooth.

4 Return the dough to the bowl, cover with an oiled sheet of plastic wrap, and leave to rise for 30 minutes, or until doubled in size.

5 Remove the dough from the bowl. Knead the dough for 2 minutes.

6 Using a rolling pin, roll out the dough to form a round, then place it on a greased cookie sheet, pushing out the edges until even. The dough should be no more than ¼ inch thick because it will rise during cooking.

7 Generously spread the sun-dried tomato paste over the dough, then add spoonfuls of ricotta.

8 Cut the sun-dried tomatoes into strips and arrange them on top of the pizza.

9 Sprinkle the thyme, and salt and pepper to taste over the top of the pizza. Bake in a preheated oven at 400°F for 30 minutes, or until the crust is golden. Serve hot.

COOK'S TIP

The dough for crispy-based pizzas should be rolled out as thinly as possible.

Mushroom Pizza

Juicy mushrooms and stringy mozzarella top this tomato-based pizza.
Use exotic mushrooms or a combination of mushrooms.

Serves 4

INGREDIENTS

1 portion Basic Pizza Dough (see page 196)

TOPPING:
14 ounce can chopped tomatoes
2 garlic cloves, crushed
1 tsp dried basil
1 tbsp olive oil

2 tbsp tomato paste
7 ounces mushrooms
$1^1/_2$ cups grated mozzarella cheese,
salt and pepper
basil leaves, to garnish

1 Place the yeast and sugar in a bowl and mix with 4 tbsp of the water. Set the yeast mixture aside in a warm place for 15 minutes, or until frothy.

2 Mix the flour with the salt and make a well in the center. Add the oil, the yeast mixture, and the remaining water. Using a wooden spoon, mix to form a dough.

3 Turn the dough out onto a floured surface and knead for 4–5 minutes, or until smooth. Return the dough to the bowl, cover with an oiled sheet of plastic wrap, and set aside to rise for 30 minutes, or until doubled in size.

4 Remove the dough from the bowl. Knead the dough for 2 minutes. Using a rolling pin, roll out the dough to form an oval or a circular shape, then place it on a greased cookie sheet, pushing out the edges until even. The dough should be no more than ¼ inch thick because it will rise during cooking.

5 Using a sharp knife, cut the mushrooms into slices.

6 To make the topping, place the tomatoes, garlic, dried basil, olive oil, and salt and pepper in a large pan and simmer for 20 minutes, or until the sauce has thickened. Stir in the tomato paste and cool slightly.

7 Spread the sauce over the base of the pizza, top with the sliced mushrooms, and scatter over the mozzarella.

8 Bake in a preheated oven at 400°F for 25 minutes. Just before serving, garnish with fresh basil leaves.

Mini Pizzas

*Pizette, as they are known in Italy, are tiny pizzas. This quantity will make
8 individual pizzas, or 16 cocktail pizzas to go with drinks.*

Makes 8

INGREDIENTS

1 portion Basic Pizza Dough (see
  page 196)

TOPPING:
2 zucchini
3¹/₂ ounces tomato sauce
3 cups diced pancetta

¹/₂ cup pitted black olives, chopped
1 tbsp mixed dried herbs
2 tbsp olive oil

1 Place the yeast and sugar in a bowl and mix with 4 tbsp of the water. Set the yeast mixture aside in a warm place for 15 minutes, or until frothy.

2 Mix the flour with the salt and make a well in the center. Add the oil, the yeast mixture, and the remaining water. Using a wooden spoon, mix to form a dough.

3 Turn the dough out onto a floured surface and knead for 4–5 minutes, or until smooth. Return the dough to the bowl, cover with an oiled sheet of plastic wrap, and set aside to rise for

30 minutes, or until doubled in size.

4 Knead the dough for 2 minutes and divide it into 8 balls. Roll out each portion thinly to form rounds or squares, then place them on a greased cookie sheet, pushing out the edges until even. The dough should be no more than ¹/₄ inch thick because it will rise during cooking.

5 To make the topping, grate the zucchini finely. Cover with absorbent paper towels and let stand for 10 minutes to absorb some of the juices.

6 Spread 2–3 teaspoons of the tomato sauce over the pizza bases and top each with the grated zucchini, pancetta, and olives. Season with freshly ground black pepper and a sprinkling of mixed dried herbs. Drizzle with olive oil.

7 Bake in a preheated oven at 400°F for 15 minutes, or until crispy. Season and serve hot.

Pizza with Tomato Sauce & Roasted Bell Peppers

This pizza, which is similar to the French Pissaladière, *is made with a pastry base flavored with cheese and topped with a delicious tomato sauce and roasted bell peppers.*

Serves 4

INGREDIENTS

2 cups all-purpose flour
1/2 cup butter, diced
1/2 tsp salt
1/2 cup grated Parmesan cheese
1 egg, beaten
2 tbsp cold water

2 tbsp olive oil
1 large onion, finely chopped
1 garlic clove, chopped
14 ounce can chopped tomatoes
4 tbsp concentrated tomato paste
1 red bell pepper, seeded and halved

5 sprigs thyme, stalks removed
6 black olives, pitted and halved

1 Sift the flour and rub in the butter until the mixture resembles bread crumbs. Stir in the salt and 2 tablespoons of the Parmesan. Add the egg and 1 tablespoon of the water and mix with a round-bladed knife. Add more water as necessary to make a soft dough. Cover with plastic wrap and chill for 30 minutes.

2 Meanwhile, heat the oil in a skillet and sauté the onions and garlic for about 5 minutes, or until golden. Add the tomatoes and cook for 8–10 minutes. Stir in the tomato paste.

3 Place the bell peppers, skin side up, on a cookie sheet and cook under a preheated broiler for 15 minutes, until charred. Place in a plastic bag and let sweat for 10 minutes. Peel off the skin and slice the flesh into thin strips.

4 Roll out the dough to fit a 9-inch loose-base fluted flan pan. Line with foil and bake in a preheated oven at 400°F for 10 minutes, or until just set. Remove the foil and bake for a further 5 minutes, until lightly golden. Cool slightly.

5 Spoon the tomato sauce evenly over the pastry base and top with the bell peppers, thyme, olives, and remaining Parmesan cheese. Bake for about 15 minutes, until the pastry is crisp. Serve warm or cold.

Calzone

A calzone can have many different fillings.
Here, cured meats mix well with mozzarella and Parmesan cheese.

Makes 4 large or 8 small calzone

INGREDIENTS

1 portion of Basic Pizza Dough (see
   page 196)
freshly grated Parmesan cheese,
   to serve

TOPPING:
2³/₄ ounces mortadella or other
   Italian pork sausage, chopped
¹/₂ cup chopped Italian sausage
1³/₄ ounces Parmesan cheese, sliced

3¹/₂ ounces mozzarella cheese, cut
   into chunks
2 tomatoes, diced
4 tbsp fresh oregano
salt and pepper

1 Place the yeast and sugar in a bowl and mix with 4 tbsp of the water. Set the yeast mixture aside in a warm place for 15 minutes, or until frothy.

2 Mix the flour with the salt and make a well in the center. Add the oil, the yeast mixture, and the remaining water. Using a wooden spoon, mix to form a dough.

3 Turn the dough out onto a floured surface and knead for 4–5 minutes, or until smooth. Return the dough to the bowl, cover with an oiled sheet of plastic wrap and set aside to rise for 30 minutes, or until doubled in size.

4 Knead the dough for 2 minutes and divide it into 4 pieces. Roll out each portion thinly to form rounds. Place them on a greased cookie sheet. The dough should be no more than ¹/₄ inch thick because it will rise during cooking.

5 To make the topping, place both Italian sausages, the Parmesan, and the mozzarella on one side of each round. Top with the tomatoes and oregano. Season to taste with salt and pepper.

6 Brush around the edges of the dough with a little water, then fold over the rounds to form a turnover shape. Squeeze the edges together to seal so that none of the filling leaks out during cooking.

7 Bake in a preheated oven at 400°F for 10–15 minutes, or until golden. If you are making the smaller pizzas, reduce the cooking time to 8–10 minutes. Serve the calzone with freshly grated Parmesan cheese.

Pizza with Creamy Ham & Cheese Sauce

This is a traditional pizza that uses a pastry case and béchamel sauce to make a type of savory flan. Grating the pastry gives it a lovely nutty texture.

Serves 4

INGREDIENTS

9 ounces flaky pastry dough,
   well chilled
3 tbsp butter
1 red onion, chopped
1 garlic clove, chopped
$1/3$ cup strong flour

$1^1/4$ cups milk
$2/3$ cup finely grated Parmesan
   cheese, plus extra for sprinkling
2 eggs, hard-boiled, cut
   into quarters

$3^1/2$ ounces Italian pork sausage,
   such as Feline salami, cut into
   strips
salt and pepper
sprigs of fresh thyme, to garnish

1 Fold the sheet of flaky pastry in half and coarsely grate it into 4 individual flan pans, 4 inches across. Using a floured fork, press the pastry flakes down lightly so that they are even, there are no holes, and the pastry comes up the sides of the pan.

2 Line with aluminum foil and bake in a preheated oven at 425°F for 10 minutes. Reduce the heat to 400°F, remove the foil, and cook for a further 15 minutes, or until the pastry shells are a golden color and set.

3 Heat the butter in a pan. Add the onion and garlic and sauté for 5–6 minutes, or until softened.

4 Add the flour, stirring well to coat the onions. Gradually stir in the milk to make a thick sauce. Season well with salt and pepper, and then stir in the Parmesan cheese. Do not reheat once the cheese has been added or the sauce will become stringy.

5 Spread the sauce over the pastry shells. Decorate with the egg and strips of sausage.

6 Sprinkle with a little extra Parmesan cheese, return to the oven and bake for 5 minutes, just to heat through.

7 Serve immediately, garnished with sprigs of fresh thyme.

COOK'S TIP

This pizza is just as good cold, but do not prepare it too far in advance or the pastry will become soggy.

Olive Oil Bread with Cheese

This flat cheese bread is sometimes called focaccia. *It is delicious served with* antipasto *or simply on its own.*

Makes 1 loaf

INGREDIENTS

$^1/_2$ ounce dried yeast
1 tsp sugar
$1^1/_8$ cups lukewarm water

3 cups strong flour
1 tsp salt
3 tbsp olive oil

7 ounces pecorino cheese, cubed
$1^1/_2$ tsp fennel seeds, lightly crushed

1 Mix the yeast with the sugar and 8 tbsp of the water. Set aside to ferment in a warm place for about 15 minutes.

2 Mix the flour with the salt. Add 1 tbsp of the oil, the yeast mixture, and the remaining water to form a smooth dough. Knead the dough for 4 minutes.

3 Divide the dough into 2 equal portions. Roll out each portion to a form a round $^1/_4$ inch thick. Place 1 round on a cookie sheet. Scatter the cheese and half the fennel seeds evenly on top.

4 Place the second round on top and squeeze the edges together to seal, so that the filling does not leak during cooking.

5 Using a sharp knife, make a few slashes in the top of the dough and brush with the remaining olive oil.

6 Sprinkle with the remaining fennel seeds and set aside to rise for 20–30 minutes.

7 Bake in a preheated oven at 400°F for 30 minutes, or until golden. Serve immediately or cool before serving.

COOK'S TIP

Pecorino is a hard, quite salty cheese, which is sold in most supermarkets and Italian delicatessens. If you cannot obtain pecorino, use strong cheddar or Parmesan cheese instead.

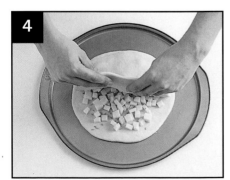

Roman Focaccia

Roman focaccia *makes a delicious snack on its own or serve it with cured meats and salad for a quick supper.*

Makes 16 squares

INGREDIENTS

$^1/_4$ ounce dried yeast
1 tsp sugar
$1^1/_4$ cups lukewarm water

4 cups strong white flour
2 tsp salt
3 tbsp rosemary, chopped
2 tbsp olive oil

1 pound mixed red and white onions,
  sliced into rings
4 garlic cloves, sliced

1 Place the yeast and the sugar in a small bowl and mix with 8 tablespoons of the water. Set aside to ferment in a warm place for 15 minutes.

2 Mix the flour with the salt in a large bowl. Add the yeast mixture, half the rosemary, and the remaining water and mix to form a smooth dough. Knead the dough for 4 minutes.

3 Cover the dough with oiled plastic wrap and set aside to rise for 30 minutes, or until doubled in size.

4 Meanwhile, heat the oil in a large pan. Add the onions and garlic and sauté for 5 minutes or until softened. Cover the pan and continue to cook for a further 7–8 minutes, or until the onions are lightly caramelized.

5 Remove the dough from the bowl and knead it again for 1–2 minutes.

6 Roll the dough out to form a square shape. The dough should be no more than $^1/_4$ inch thick because it will rise during cooking. Place the dough onto a

cookie sheet, pushing out the edges until even.

7 Spread the onions over the dough, and sprinkle with the remaining rosemary.

8 Bake in a preheated oven at 400°F for 25–30 minutes, or until golden. Cut into 16 squares and serve immediately.

Sun-dried Tomato Loaf

*This delicious tomato bread is great with cheese or
soup, or to make an unusual sandwich.*

Makes 1 loaf

INGREDIENTS

$^1/_4$ ounce dried yeast	4 cups strong white flour	2 tbsp sun-dried tomato paste
1 tsp sugar	1 tsp salt	12 sun-dried tomatoes, cut
$1^1/_4$ cups lukewarm water	2 tsp dried basil	into strips

1 Place the yeast and sugar in a small bowl and mix with 8 tablespoons of the water. Set aside to ferment in a warm place for 15 minutes.

2 Place the flour in a bowl and stir in the salt. Make a well in the dry ingredients and add the basil, the yeast mixture, tomato paste, and half the remaining water. Using a wooden spoon, draw the flour into the liquid and mix to form a dough, adding the rest of the water gradually.

3 Turn out the dough onto a floured surface and knead for 5 minutes, or until smooth. Cover with oiled plastic wrap and set aside in a warm place to rise for about 30 minutes, or until doubled in size.

4 Lightly grease a 2-pound loaf pan.

5 Remove the dough from the bowl and knead in the sun-dried tomatoes. Knead again for 2–3 minutes.

6 Place the dough in the pan and set aside to rise for 30–40 minutes. Once it has doubled in size again, bake in a preheated oven at 375°F for 30–35 minutes, or until golden and the base sounds hollow when tapped.

COOK'S TIP

You could make mini sun-dried tomato loaves for children. Divide the dough into 8 equal portions, set aside to rise, and bake in mini-loaf pans for 20 minutes. Alternatively, make 12 small rounds, leave to rise, and bake as rolls for 12–15 minutes.

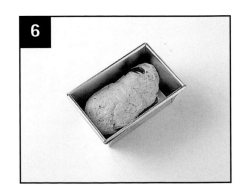

Roasted Bell Pepper Bread

Bell peppers become sweet and mild when they are roasted and make this bread delicious.

Serves 4

INGREDIENTS

1 red bell pepper, halved and seeded
1 yellow bell pepper, halved and
   seeded
2 sprigs rosemary

1 tbsp olive oil
$^{1}/_{4}$ ounce dried yeast
1 tsp sugar
$1^{1}/_{4}$ cups lukewarm water

4 cups strong white flour
1 tsp salt

1 Grease a 9-inch, deep round cake pan with a little butter or margarine.

2 Place the bell peppers and rosemary in a shallow roasting pan. Sprinkle with the oil and roast in a preheated oven at 400°F for 20 minutes, or until slightly charred. Remove the skin from the bell peppers and cut the flesh into slices.

3 Place the yeast and sugar in a small bowl and mix with 8 tablespoons of lukewarm water. Set the yeast mixture aside to ferment in a warm place for about 15 minutes.

4 Mix the flour and salt together in a large bowl. Stir in the yeast mixture and the remaining water and mix to form a smooth dough.

5 Knead the dough for about 5 minutes. Cover with oiled plastic wrap and set aside to rise for about 30 minutes, or until doubled in size.

6 Cut the dough into 3 equal portions. Roll the portions into rounds slightly larger than the cake pan.

7 Place 1 round in the base of the pan so that it reaches up the sides of the pan by about $^{3}/_{4}$ inch. Top with half the bell pepper mixture.

8 Place the second round of dough on top, followed by the remaining bell pepper mixture. Place the last round of dough on top, pushing the edges of the dough down the sides of the pan.

9 Cover the dough with oiled plastic wrap and set aside to rise for 30–40 minutes. Place in the preheated oven and bake for 45 minutes, until golden and the base sounds hollow when lightly tapped. Serve warm.

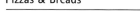

Green Easter Pie

This traditional Easter risotto pie is from Piedmont in northern Italy.
Serve it warm or chilled in slices.

Serves 4

INGREDIENTS

2 tbsp olive oil
1 onion, chopped
2 garlic cloves, chopped
1 cup risotto rice
3 cups hot chicken or vegetable stock
$^1/_2$ cup white wine

$^2/_3$ cup grated Parmesan cheese
$^3/_4$ cup frozen peas, thawed
3 ounces arugula
2 tomatoes, diced
4 eggs, beaten
3 tbsp fresh marjoram, chopped

1 cup bread crumbs
salt and pepper

1 Lightly grease and then line the base of a 9-inch, deep cake pan.

2 Using a sharp knife, roughly chop the arugula.

3 Heat the oil in a large skillet. Add the onion and garlic and sauté for 4–5 minutes, or until the onion has softened.

4 Add the rice to the mixture in the skillet, mix well to combine, then begin adding the stock a ladleful at a time. Wait until all the stock has been completely absorbed before adding another ladleful of liquid.

5 Continue to cook the mixture, adding the wine, until the rice is tender. This will take at least 15 minutes.

6 Stir in the Parmesan cheese, peas, arugula, tomatoes, eggs, and 2 tablespoons of the marjoram. Season to taste with salt and pepper.

7 Spoon the risotto into the pan and level the surface by pressing down with the back of a wooden spoon.

8 Top with the bread crumbs and the remaining marjoram.

9 Bake in a preheated oven at 350°F for 30 minutes, or until set. Cut into slices and serve immediately or cool and chill.

Spinach & Ricotta Pie

This puff pastry pie looks impressive and is actually very easy to make. Serve it hot or cold.

Serves 4

INGREDIENTS

8 ounces spinach
$^1/_4$ cup pine nuts
$^1/_2$ cup ricotta cheese

2 large eggs, beaten
$^1/_2$ cup ground almonds
$^2/_3$ cup grated Parmesan cheese

9 ounces puff pastry dough, thawed
  if frozen
1 small egg, beaten

1 Rinse the spinach, place in a large saucepan, and cook for 4-5 minutes, until wilted. Drain thoroughly. When the spinach is cool enough to handle, squeeze out the excess liquid.

2 Place the pine nuts on a cookie sheet and lightly toast under a preheated broiler for 2–3 minutes, or until golden.

3 Place the ricotta cheese, spinach and eggs in a bowl and mix together. Add the pine nuts, beat well, then stir in the ground almonds and grated Parmesan cheese.

4 Roll out the puff pastry dough and make 2 x 8-inch squares. Trim the edges, reserving the dough trimmings.

5 Place 1 dough square on a cookie sheet. Spoon the spinach mixture on top, keeping within $^1/_2$ inch of the edge of the dough square. Brush the edges with beaten egg and place the second square over the top.

6 Using a round-bladed knife, press the edges together by tapping along the sealed edge. Use the dough trimmings to make leaves to decorate the pie.

7 Brush the pie with the beaten egg to glaze and bake in a preheated oven at 425°F for 10 minutes. Reduce the oven temperature to 375°F and bake for a further 25–30 minutes. Serve hot.

COOK'S TIP

Spinach is very nutritious as it is full of iron—this is particularly important for women and elderly people who may lack this in their diet.

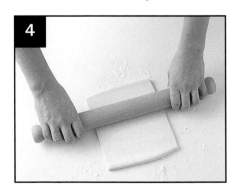

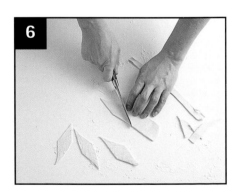

Desserts

The Italians love their desserts, but when there is a special gathering or celebration, then a special effort is made and the delicacies appear. The Sicilians are said to have the sweetest tooth of all, and many Italian desserts are thought to have originated there. You have to go a very long way to beat a Sicilian ice cream—they truly are the best in the world!

Fresh fruit also features in many Italian desserts— oranges are often peeled and served whole, marinated in a fragrant syrup and liqueur. For a deliciously fruity dessert, try Sicilian Orange & Almond Cake, Orange & Grapefruit Salad, or the intoxicating flavor of Marinated Peaches.

Chocolate, too, is popular in Italy—sample Rich Chocolate Loaf and the all-time favorite tiramisu for a deliciously wicked end to a meal. Whatever your preference, there is sure to be an Italian dessert to tempt and satisfy you—you'll never be disappointed!

Italian Bread Pudding

This deliciously rich pudding is cooked with cream and apples and is delicately flavored with orange.

Serves 4

INGREDIENTS

1 tbsp butter
2 small eating apples, peeled, cored, and sliced into rings
$^1/_4$ cup sugar

2 tbsp white wine
$3^1/_2$ ounces bread, sliced with crusts removed (slightly stale French baguette is ideal)

$1^1/_4$ cups light cream
2 eggs, beaten
pared rind of 1 orange, cut into matchsticks

1 Lightly grease a 2-pint, deep ovenproof dish with the butter.

2 Arrange the apple rings in the base of the dish. Sprinkle half the sugar over the apples.

3 Pour the wine over the apple slices. Add the slices of bread, pushing them down with your hands to flatten them slightly.

4 Mix the cream with the eggs, the remaining sugar, and the orange rind, and pour the mixture over the bread. Set aside to soak for 30 minutes.

5 Bake the pudding in a preheated oven at 350°F for 25 minutes, until golden and set. Serve warm.

COOK'S TIP

Light cream is the type of cream most commonly used for cooking. However, this type of cream should not be boiled as it will curdle. Also, always add hot liquids to the cream rather than the cream to the liquids, in order to avoid curdling. Light cream has an 18 percent fat content.

VARIATION

Try adding dried fruit, such as apricots, cherries, or dates, to the pudding.

Tuscan Pudding

*These baked mini-ricotta puddings are delicious served warm
or chilled and will keep in the refrigerator for 3–4 days.*

Serves 4

INGREDIENTS

1 tbsp butter
1/2 cup mixed dried fruit
1 1/8 cups ricotta cheese

3 egg yolks
1/4 cup superfine sugar
1 tsp cinnamon

finely grated rind of 1 orange, plus
extra to decorate
crème fraîche to serve

1 Lightly grease 4 mini ovenproof bowls or ramekin dishes with the butter.

2 Put the dried fruit in a bowl and cover with warm water. Set aside to soak for 10 minutes.

3 Beat the ricotta cheese with the egg yolks in a bowl. Stir in the superfine sugar, cinnamon, and orange rind and mix well to combine.

4 Drain the dried fruit in a strainer set over a bowl. Mix the drained fruit with the ricotta cheese mixture.

5 Spoon the mixture into the bowls or ramekin dishes.

6 Bake in a preheated oven at 350°F for 15 minutes. The tops should be firm to the touch, but not brown.

7 Decorate the puddings with grated orange rind. Serve warm or chilled with a spoon of crème fraîche.

VARIATION

*Use the dried fruit of your choice for
this delicious recipe.*

COOK'S TIP

*Crème fraîche has a slightly sour,
nutty taste and is very thick. It is
suitable for cooking, but has the
same fat content as heavy cream. It
can be made by stirring cultured
buttermilk into heavy cream and
refrigerating overnight.*

Cream Custards

Individual pan-cooked cream custards are flavored with nutmeg and topped with caramelized orange sticks.

Serves 4

INGREDIENTS

2 cups light cream
2 tbsp superfine sugar
1 orange

2 tsp grated nutmeg
3 large eggs, beaten
1 tbsp honey

1 tsp cinnamon

1 Place the cream and sugar in a large nonstick saucepan and heat gently, stirring, until the sugar caramelizes.

2 Finely grate half the orange rind and add it to the pan, together with the nutmeg.

3 Add the eggs to the mixture in the pan and cook over a low heat for 10–15 minutes, stirring constantly. The custard will eventually thicken.

4 Strain the custard through a fine strainer into 4 shallow serving dishes. Chill in the refrigerator for 2 hours.

5 Meanwhile, pare the remaining orange rind and cut it into matchsticks.

6 Place the honey and cinnamon in a pan with 2 tablespoons water and heat gently. Add the orange rind to the pan and cook for 2–3 minutes, stirring, until the mixture has caramelized.

7 Pour the mixture into a bowl and separate the orange sticks. Cool until set.

8 Once the custards have set, decorate them with the caramelized orange rind and serve.

COOK'S TIP

The cream custards will keep for 1–2 days in the refrigerator. Decorate with the caramelized orange rind just before serving.

Sicilian Orange & Almond Cake

This is a light and tangy citrus cake better eaten as a dessert than as a cake.
It is especially good served after a large meal.

Serves 8

INGREDIENTS

4 eggs, separated
$^3/_4$ cup superfine sugar, plus 2 tsp for
   the cream
finely grated rind and juice of
   2 oranges

finely grated rind and juice of
   1 lemon
1 cup ground almonds
$^1/_4$ cup self-rising flour

$^3/_4$ cup heavy cream
1 tsp cinnamon
$^1/_4$ cup slivered almonds, toasted
confectioner's sugar, to dust

1 Lightly grease and line the base of a 7-inch round, deep cake pan.

2 Blend the egg yolks with the sugar until the mixture is thick and creamy. Beat half the orange rind and all the lemon rind into the egg yolks.

3 Mix the juice from both oranges and the lemon with the ground almonds and stir into the egg yolks. The mixture will become quite runny at this point. Fold in the flour.

4 Whisk the egg whites until stiff and gently fold into the egg yolk mixture.

5 Pour the mixture into the prepared cake pan and bake in a preheated oven at 350°F for 35–40 minutes, until golden and springy to the touch. Cool in the pan for 10 minutes and then turn out. It is likely to sink slightly at this stage.

6 Beat the cream to form soft peaks. Stir in the remaining orange rind, cinnamon, and sugar.

7 Once the cake is cold, cover with the toasted almonds, dust with confectioner's sugar, and serve with the cream.

VARIATION

You could serve this cake with a syrup. Boil the juice and finely grated rind of 2 oranges, 6 tbsp superfine sugar, and 2 tbsp water for 5–6 minutes, until slightly thickened. Stir in 1 tbsp of orange liqueur just before serving.

Orange & Grapefruit Salad

*Sliced citrus fruits with a delicious almond and honey dressing
make an unusual and refreshing dessert.*

Serves 4

INGREDIENTS

2 grapefruit, pink or plain
4 oranges
pared rind and juice of 1 lime

4 tbsp clear honey
2 tbsp warm water

1 sprig mint, roughly chopped
$^1/_2$ cup chopped walnuts

1 Using a sharp knife, slice the top and bottom from the grapefruit, then slice away the rest of the skin and pith.

2 Cut between each segment of the grapefruit to remove the fleshy part only.

3 Using a sharp knife, slice the top and bottom from the oranges, then slice away the rest of the skin and pith.

4 Cut between each segment of the oranges to remove the fleshy part. Add to the grapefruit.

5 Place the lime rind, 2 tablespoons of lime juice, the honey, and the warm water in a small bowl. Beat with a fork to mix the dressing.

6 Pour the dressing over the segmented fruit, add the chopped mint, and mix well. Chill in the refrigerator for 2 hours for the flavors to mingle.

7 Place the chopped walnuts on a cookie sheet. Lightly toast the walnuts under a preheated broiler for 2–3 minutes, until golden brown.

8 Sprinkle the toasted walnuts over the fruit and serve.

VARIATION

Instead of the walnuts, you could sprinkle toasted almonds, cashews, hazelnuts, or pecans over the fruit, if you prefer.

Zabaglione

This well-known dish is really a light, but rich egg mousse flavored with Marsala.

Serves 4

INGREDIENTS

5 egg yolks
$\frac{1}{2}$ cup superfine sugar

$\frac{2}{3}$ cup Marsala or sweet sherry
fresh fruit or amaretti cookies, to
serve (optional)

1 Place the egg yolks in a large mixing bowl.

2 Add the superfine sugar to the egg yolks and beat well until the mixture is thick and very pale and has doubled in volume.

3 Place the bowl containing the egg yolk and sugar mixture over a saucepan of gently simmering water.

4 Add the Marsala or sherry to the egg yolk and sugar mixture and continue beating until the foam mixture becomes warm. This process may take as long as 10 minutes.

5 Pour the mixture, which should be frothy and light, into 4 wine glasses.

6 Serve the zabaglione warm with fresh fruit or amaretti cookies if you wish.

VARIATION

Iced or Semifreddo Zabaglione *can be made by following the method here, then continuing to beat the foam while standing the bowl in cold water. Beat $\frac{2}{3}$ cup heavy cream until it just holds its shape. Fold into the foam and freeze for about 2 hours, until just frozen.*

VARIATION

Any other type of liqueur may be used instead of the Marsala or sweet sherry, if you prefer. Serve soft fruits, such as strawberries or raspberries, with the zabaglione— it's a delicious combination!

Sweet Mascarpone Mousse

*A sweet cream cheese dessert that complements the
tartness of fresh summer fruits rather well.*

Serves 4

INGREDIENTS

2 cups mascarpone cheese ¹/₂ cup superfine sugar 4 egg yolks	14 ounces frozen summer fruits, such as raspberries and red currants	red currants, to garnish amaretti cookies, to serve

1 Place the mascarpone cheese in a large mixing bowl. Using a wooden spoon, beat the mascarpone cheese until very smooth.

2 Stir the egg yolks and sugar into the mascarpone cheese, mixing well. Chill in the refrigerator for about 1 hour.

3 Spoon a layer of the mascarpone mixture into the bottom of 4 individual serving dishes. Spoon a layer of the summer fruits on top. Repeat the layers in the same order, reserving some of the mascarpone mixture for the top.

4 Chill the mousses in the refrigerator for about 20 minutes. The fruits should still be slightly frozen.

5 Serve the mascarpone mousses with amaretti cookies.

COOK'S TIP

Mascarpone (sometimes spelled mascherpone) is a soft, creamy cheese from Italy. It is becoming increasingly available, and you should have no difficulty finding it in your local supermarket, or Italian delicatessen.

VARIATION

Try adding 3 tablespoons of your favorite liqueur to the mascarpone cheese mixture in step 1, if desired.

Lemon Mascarpone Cheesecake

The mascarpone gives this baked cheesecake a wonderfully tangy flavor.

Serves 8

INGREDIENTS

1¹/₂ tbsp unsalted butter
2 cups crushed ginger snaps
2 tbsp preserved ginger
2¹/₄ cups mascarpone cheese

finely grated rind and juice of
  2 lemons
1 cup superfine sugar

2 large eggs, separated
fruit coulis (see Cook's Tip), to serve

1 Grease and line the base of a 10-inch springform cake pan or loose-bottomed pan.

2 Melt the butter in a pan and stir in the crushed cookies and chopped ginger. Use the mixture to line the pan, pressing the mixture about ¹/₂ inch up the sides.

3 Beat together the cheese, lemon rind and juice, sugar, and egg yolks until smooth.

4 Whisk the egg whites until they are stiff and fold into the cheese and lemon mixture, blending well.

5 Pour the mixture into the cookie shell in the pan and bake in a preheated oven at 350°F for 35–45 minutes, until just set. Don't worry if it cracks or sinks—this is quite normal.

6 Leave the cheesecake in the pan to cool. Serve with fruit coulis (see Cook's Tip).

VARIATION

Ricotta cheese can be used instead of the mascarpone to make an equally delicious cheesecake. However, it should be rubbed through a strainer before use to remove any lumps.

COOK'S TIP

Fruit coulis can be made by cooking 14 ounces fruit, such as blueberries, for 5 minutes with 2 tablespoons of water. Strain the mixture, then stir in 1 tablespoon (or more to taste) of sifted confectioner's sugar. Cool before serving.

Tiramisu

This is a traditional chocolate dessert from Italy, although at one time it was known as Zuppa Inglese *because it was a favorite with the English society living in Florence in the 1800s.*

Serves 6

INGREDIENTS

10^1/$_2$ ounces dark chocolate
1^3/$_4$ cups mascarpone cheese
^{2}/$_3$ cup heavy cream, whipped until it
  just holds its shape

1^3/$_4$ cups black coffee with
  ^{1}/$_4$ cup superfine sugar, cooled
6 tbsp dark rum or brandy

36 lady fingers, about 14 oz
unsweetened cocoa, to dust

1 Melt the chocolate in a bowl set over a saucepan of simmering water, stirring occasionally. Leave the chocolate to cool slightly, then stir it into the mascarpone and cream.

2 Mix the coffee and rum together in a bowl. Dip the lady fingers into the mixture briefly so that they absorb the liquid, but do not become soggy and disintegrate.

3 Place 3 lady fingers on 3 serving plates.

4 Spoon a layer of the mascarpone and chocolate mixture over the lady fingers.

5 Place 3 more lady fingers on top of the mascarpone layer. Spread another layer of mascarpone and chocolate mixture and place 3 more lady fingers on top.

6 Chill the tiramisu in the refrigerator for at least 1 hour. Dust with a little unsweetened cocoa just before serving.

COOK'S TIP

Tiramisu can also be served semi-frozen, like ice cream. Freeze the tiramisu for 2 hours and serve immediately, as it defrosts very quickly.

VARIATION

Try adding ^{1}/$_2$ *cup toasted, chopped hazelnuts to the chocolate cream mixture in step 1, if desired.*

Rich Chocolate Loaf

*Another rich chocolate dessert, this loaf is very simple to make
and can be served as a morning coffee treat as well.*

Makes 16 slices

INGREDIENTS

5$^{1}/_{2}$ ounces dark chocolate
6 tbsp sweet butter
7$^{1}/_{4}$ ounce can condensed milk

2 tsp cinnamon
$^{1}/_{2}$ cup almonds,
1 cup broken amaretti cookies

$^{1}/_{4}$ cup chopped dried no-need-to-
soak apricots

1 Line a 1$^{1}/_{2}$-pound loaf
pan with a sheet of foil.

2 Using a sharp knife, roughly
chop the almonds.

3 Place the chocolate, butter,
milk, and cinnamon in a
heavy-based saucepan. Heat gently
over a low heat for 3–4 minutes,
stirring with a wooden spoon,
until the chocolate has melted.
Beat the mixture well.

4 Add the almonds, cookies,
and apricots to the chocolate
mixture in the saucepan, stirring

with a wooden spoon, until well
mixed.

5 Pour the mixture into the
prepared pan and chill in the
refrigerator for about 1 hour, or
until set.

6 Cut the rich chocolate loaf
into slices to serve.

COOK'S TIP

*To melt chocolate, first break it into
manageable pieces. The smaller the
pieces, the quicker it will melt.*

COOK'S TIP

*When baking or cooking with fat,
butter has the finest flavor. If
possible, it is best to use sweet butter
as an ingredient in puddings and
desserts, unless stated otherwise in
the recipe. Reduced fat spreads are
not suitable for cooking.*

Pear & Ginger Cake

This deliciously buttery pear and ginger cake is ideal for serving with coffee or you can serve it with cream for a delicious dessert.

Serves 4–6

INGREDIENTS

$^7/_8$ cup sweet butter, softened
$^3/_4$ cup superfine sugar
$1^1/_2$ cups self-rising flour, sifted
3 tsp ground ginger

3 eggs, beaten
1 pound eating pears, peeled, cored, and thinly sliced
1 tbsp brown sugar

ice cream or heavy cream (optional), to serve

1 Lightly grease and line the base of a deep 8-inch cake pan.

2 Using a whisk, combine $^3/_4$ cup of the butter with the superfine sugar, flour, ginger, and eggs and mix to form a smooth consistency.

3 Spoon the cake mixture into the prepared pan, leveling the surface.

4 Arrange the pear slices over the cake mixture. Sprinkle with the brown sugar and dot with the remaining butter.

5 Bake in a preheated oven at 350°F for 35–40 minutes, or until the cake is golden and feels springy to the touch.

6 Serve the pear and ginger cake warm, with ice cream or cream, if desired.

COOK'S TIP

Brown sugar is often known as Barbados sugar. It is a darker form of light brown sugar.

COOK'S TIP

To test whether the cake is cooked through, insert a knife into the center of the cake. If it comes out clean the cake is cooked through.

Peaches in White Wine

A very simple but incredibly pleasing dessert, which is especially good for a dinner party on a hot summer evening.

Serves 4

INGREDIENTS

4 large ripe peaches
2 tbsp confectioner's sugar, sifted
pared rind and juice of 1 orange

³/₄ cup medium or sweet white
   wine, chilled

1 Using a sharp knife, halve the peaches, remove the pits, and discard them. Peel the peaches, if desired. Slice the peaches into thin wedges.

2 Place the peach wedges in a glass serving bowl and sprinkle the sugar over them.

3 Using a sharp knife, pare the rind from the orange. Cut the orange rind into matchsticks, place them in a bowl of cold water, and set aside.

4 Squeeze the juice from the orange and pour it over the peaches, together with the wine.

5 Marinate the peaches in the refrigerator for at least 1 hour.

6 Remove the orange rind from the cold water and pat dry with paper towels.

7 Garnish the peaches with the strips of orange rind and serve immediately.

COOK'S TIP

There is absolutely no need to use expensive wine in this recipe, so it can be quite economical to make.

COOK'S TIP

The best way to pare the rind thinly from citrus fruits is to use a potato peeler.

Vanilla Ice Cream

Italy is synonymous with ice cream. This homemade version of real vanilla ice cream is absolutely delicious and so easy to make.

Serves 4–6

INGREDIENTS

2¹/₂ cups heavy cream
1 vanilla bean

pared rind of 1 lemon
4 eggs, beaten

2 egg, yolks
⁷/₈ cup superfine sugar

1 Place the cream in a heavy-based saucepan and heat gently, beating. Add the vanilla bean, lemon rind, eggs, and egg yolks and heat until the mixture reaches just below boiling point.

2 Reduce the heat and cook for 8–10 minutes, beating the mixture continuously, until it has thickened.

3 Stir the sugar into the cream mixture and set aside to cool.

4 Strain the cream mixture through a fine strainer.

5 Slit open the vanilla bean, scoop out the tiny black seeds, and stir them into the cream.

6 Pour the mixture into a shallow freezing container with a lid and freeze overnight, until set. Serve when required.

COOK'S TIP

Ice cream is one of the traditional dishes of Italy. Everyone eats it and there are numerous gelato stalls selling a wide variety of flavors, usually in a cone. It is also served in scoops and sliced.

COOK'S TIP

To make tutti frutti ice cream, soak ²/₃ cup mixed dried fruit, such as golden raisins, cherries, apricots, candied peel, and pineapple, in 2 tablespoons Marsala or sweet sherry for 20 minutes. Follow the method for vanilla ice cream, omitting the vanilla bean, and stir in the Marsala or sherry-soaked fruit in step 5, just before freezing.

Granita

A delightful end to a meal or a refreshing way to cleanse the palate between courses, granitas are made from slushy ice rather than frozen solid, so they need to be served very quickly.

Serves 4

INGREDIENTS

LEMON GRANITA:
3 lemons
3/4 cup lemon juice
1/2 cup superfine sugar
2 1/4 cups cold water

COFFEE GRANITA:
2 tbsp instant coffee
2 tbsp sugar
2 tbsp hot water
2 1/2 cups cold water
2 tbsp rum or brandy

1 To make lemon granita, finely grate the lemon rind. Place the lemon rind, juice, and superfine sugar in a pan. Bring the mixture to a boil and simmer for 5-6 minutes, or until thick and syrupy. Let cool.

2 Once cooled, stir in the cold water and pour into a shallow freezer container with a lid. Freeze the granita for 4–5 hours, stirring occasionally to break up the ice. Serve as a palate cleanser between dinner courses.

3 To make coffee granita, place the coffee and sugar in a bowl and pour in the hot water, stirring until dissolved.

4 Stir in the cold water and rum or brandy.

5 Pour the mixture into a shallow freezer container with a lid. Freeze the granita for at least 6 hours, stirring every 1–2 hours in order to create a grainy texture. Serve with cream after dinner, if desired.

COOK'S TIP

If you would prefer a nonalcoholic version of the coffee granita, simply omit the rum or brandy and add extra instant coffee instead.

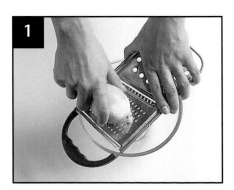

Index

Index compiled by Hilary Bird.